CHOOSING SOCIOLOGY

An Introduction to Critical Inquiry

DEENA WEINSTEIN
De Paul University
MICHAEL A. WEINSTEIN
Purdue University

David McKay Company, Inc.
New York

CHOOSING SOCIOLOGY

Copyright © 1974 and 1976 by David McKay Company, Inc.
All rights reserved, including the right to reproduce
this book, or parts thereof, in any form, except for
the inclusion of brief quotations in a review.

Chapters 1 through 5 were previously published in
Living Sociology published by David McKay Company,
Inc. in 1974.

ISBN: 0–679–30306–5
Library of Congress Catalog Card Number: 75–37485
Manufactured in the United States of America

Design by Bob Antler

CONTENTS

Introduction		v
1.	**The Human Condition**	**3**
	The Method of Self-understanding	6
	Clarification Generalization, Relativization, Commitment	
2.	**A Brief Guide to Social Thought**	**33**
	The Types of Social Thought	34
	Natural Law, Monism, Pluralism, Process	
	Social Thought in Review	54
	A Sampler of Theorists	
3.	**Sociology and Science**	**60**
	Science	61
	Accuracy	62
	Precision	70

	Consistency and Coherence	73
	Adequacy	77
	Fruitfulness	81
	Human Science	83
4.	**Method Without Madness**	**85**
	Method and Paradigm *Sociology's Approach*	87
	Diversity of Methods	90
	Classification of Methods *The Historical Method, Demographic Method, Participant Methods, Nonparticipant Observation, Survey Method, Depth Interviewing, Experimental Small Groups*	92
	Method in Review	109
5.	**Human Action**	**118**
	Restrictive Empiricism	119
	Expansive Empiricism *Directions of Human Experience*	121
	Human Action *Establishing Sociology as a Separate Discipline, The Sweep of Culture*	127
	Experience and Action	141
6.	**Sociology as a Commitment**	**142**
	The Multiversity *Paradigms*	143
	Propaganda Mills *The Mass Mind, Stimulus-Response, Other Characteristics of the Mass Mind*	148
	Sociology as Commitment *Anomie, Criticism, and "Everyday Life;" Types of Sociology; Liberation and Control; Freedom and Order; Human Science and Natural Science*	156
	Conclusion	168
	Notes	170
	Index	181

INTRODUCTION

The term "choosing sociology" has two meanings. First, one must decide whether or not to consider oneself in reference to a wider social and cultural context. All types of sociology reject the idea that the individual can be considered apart from groups, relational processes, and cultural objects. Those who believe that they are, or can be, independent of such influences have not chosen sociology; instead, they have decided to ignore the origins and consequences of their thoughts and actions. Second, once the individual has decided to take a sociological perspective, the choice remains of what kind of sociological inquiry to pursue. The idea that sociology is a process of self-understanding that involves the individual's personal encounter with multiple perspectives on the human condition is only one of many approaches to sociology. We have chosen this approach, but we realize that alternative approaches also have their intelligent and dedicated adherents.

This book is written from a particular perspective that is related to such currents as humanistic, existential, phenomenological, interactionist, reflexive, and critical sociology. Its very perspective precludes a dogmatic stance. It emphasizes the capacity for people to decide among possibilities and the desirability of expanding them. One possibility that can be chosen in sociology is a theory, method, and philosophy that denies the freedom to choose among possibilities! We take account of this option and describe it, although we also criticize it. More generally, we attempt to walk a fine line in which we defend vigorously a position that commits us to acknowledging our relativity and uncertainty, and to treating other positions sympathetically. This balancing act is one of the consequences of basing sociological inquiry on freedom.

Consonant with our approach, we believe it is important at the outset to identify the intellectual context in which this book appears. We write at a time when sociologists are becoming increasingly aware of the connection between their ideas and the social organizations in which they work. This awareness is symbolized by the widespread use of such terms as the "sociology of knowledge" and the "sociology of sociology" to identify the study of how thought about social relations and organizations relates to those very relations and organizations. We are, in part, in the tradition of such sociologists as Auguste Comte, Karl Marx, Pitirim Sorokin, Georges Gurvitch, Karl Mannheim, C. Wright Mills, and Alvin Gouldner, who attempt to trace the relations between the ideas people have about their society and the particular social groups to which they belong and the interests of these groups. We depart from the traditional sociology of knowledge in one important respect, however.

In the past, sociologists have implied or claimed that in one way or another they have been able to rise above partial and interest-bound interpretations of society, and to give an accurate statement of social reality in terms of the major social groups, their relations, and their principles of organization. We believe that contemporary sociology should not try to cut through the web of competing interpretations of human existence until it reaches a solid core of social fact. Instead, we describe a way in which people can move through the competing interpretations, understand and appreciate each of them, and create a perspective that will aid them in preserving or transforming their social relations according to values they have chosen to realize. This is just another way of saying that we do not have access to any absolute truth—religious, political, sociological, or psychological.

It is also something more. We believe that, while there is neither

Introduction vii

a bedrock of social fact nor a mountaintop for objective contemplation, a process exists for improving one's grasp of social relations by discovering the various groups with which one might identify, understanding their projects and interests, seeing how these groups relate to other groups, and making commitments to act on the basis of widened understanding. This means that we will not tell people what side they should be on in social conflicts or what side will necessarily win. We can do no more than present the best analysis we can devise through our own processes of critical comparison, and then make it clear which side we are on and why. This is how we understand the "sociology of knowledge" tradition in contemporary social science.

We are somewhat hampered in realizing our purpose of expanding possibilities by the structure of the language, by the things people expect to derive from a book, and indeed by the structure of a book itself. The English language, in its present form, hinders us because there are viewpoints we would like to express that are not communicated easily. For example, more often than not, the words "he" and "his" appear in the text when we are referring to the singular third-person subject (the abstract human being). This general usage of the masculine third person for the human third person has an obvious bias. It may (and has) led people to believe that only men are significant in social life and that only men should reflect upon social relations. This is contrary to our belief that both women and men must share equally in a human process of growth and inquiry. Yet, for the most part, we have adopted ordinary usage of the language and avoided strategies that would have made the presentation stilted or awkward, and might have distracted the reader from other insights. In parts of the text we have tried to use the third-person plural, which in English is neutral but still rather cumbersome. We avoided the use of "man" to refer to human being, and "mankind" to refer to humanity, but the language prohibited us from being as human as we desired. Perhaps in the future English will develop gender-neutral terms, but for us to coin such terms (e.g., *shis* for his/her) would be distracting.

What people expect to derive from a book also hampered us. It probably does not matter how much we insist upon the relativity of our position; many people will embrace it as a creed or react against it as a faith. People often expect a book either to tell them the truth about something or to confirm their prejudices. Our book does neither, yet it may appear to some to do both.

Finally, we have been limited by the structure of a book itself. The print medium is at its best when describing a particular point of view and where only one-way communication is possible. Conversations are bilateral or multilateral, in the sense that a number of people speaking with one another can simultaneously work out several perspectives. Books, however, are unilateral—the authors present their ideas, and the readers have no opportunity to respond immediately and present different possibilities. Thus we return again to the theme that we encourage the reader to take an active responsibility for her image of society: to try to clarify her beliefs, compare them to our perspective, and choose the ways she will commit herself to preserving or transforming social relations. We ask her not to respond passively to our viewpoint but to test it in her own life. (And this applies to *him* as well as to *her!*)

Cook and Tippecanoe
Counties, 1976

To the triumph of criticism over apology

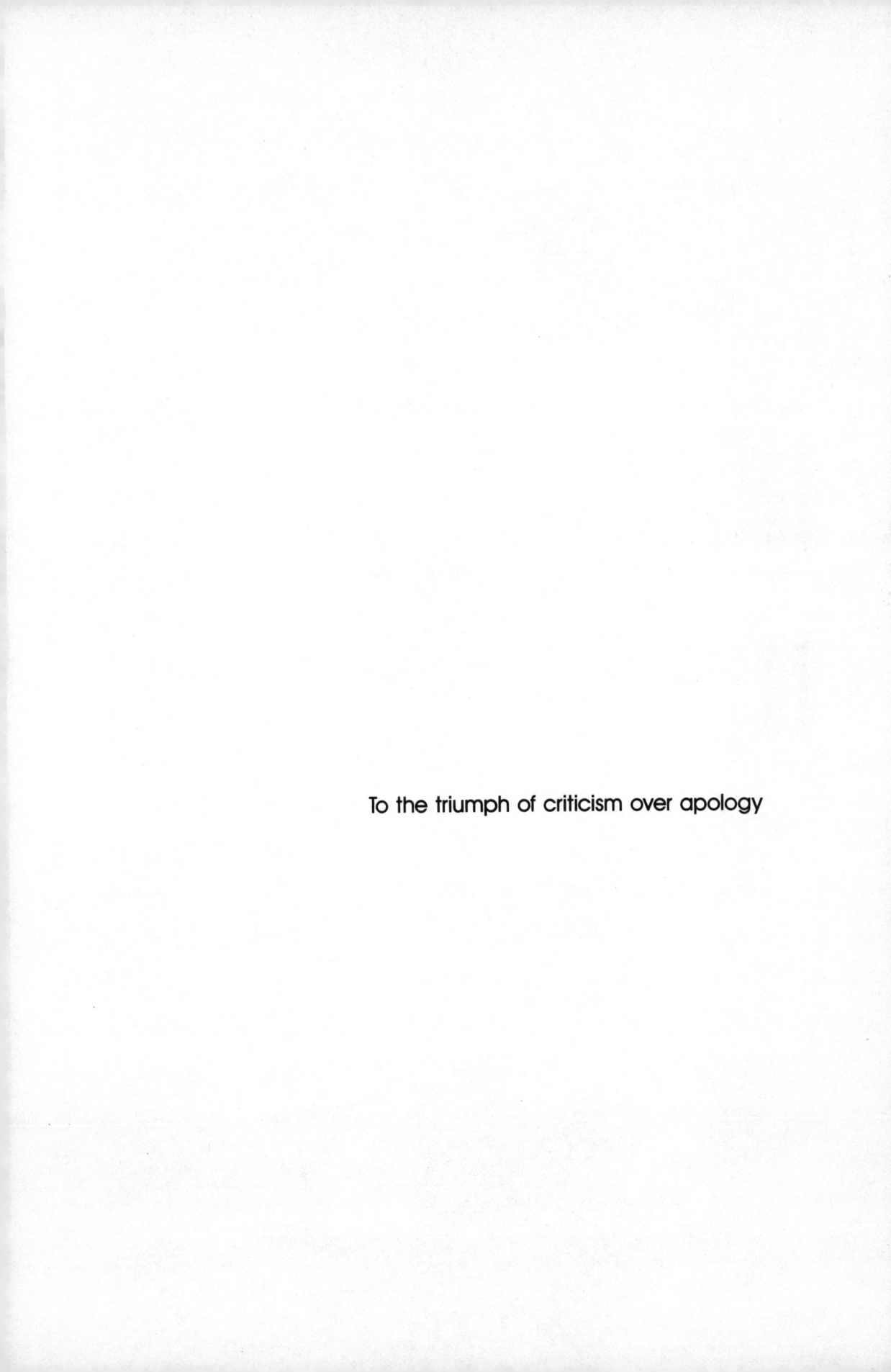

CHOOSING SOCIOLOGY

THE HUMAN CONDITION

The twentieth century is an age of contrasts, a time of beginnings and endings. At the very time when some people speak hopefully about the possibilities of a world without war and poverty, others warn of impending disaster through nuclear warfare or famine. The spread of the scientific method into new areas of human experience is extolled in some quarters, while elsewhere growing numbers of people experiment with witchcraft and astrology. Suburban homes are replete with electrical appliances, while the shacks of the rural poor may not even have indoor plumbing. Millions of human beings spend their working lives in vast organizations whose operations cannot be understood by any single individual, but return after work to the nuclear family, the smallest social unit yet devised. Depending upon the slice of experience being presented at the moment, the human condition is one of promise or peril. Bertrand Russell has expressed this twentieth-century mentality: "I see, in my mind's eye, a world of glory and joy, a world where minds expand, where hope remains undimmed, and what is noble is no longer condemned as treachery to this or that paltry aim. All this can happen if we will let it happen. It rests with our generation to decide between this vision and an end decreed by folly."[1]

It is by no means certain that the present generation will determine whether humanity progresses to a new expansion of freedom or commits collective suicide. More than one generation in the twentieth century has already found itself torn between promise and peril, and has left the issue unresolved. This uncertainty may continue for many decades into the future. What is important, however, is that many people in the twentieth century have felt that they were at the crossroads between despair and hope. Nietzsche likened human existence to a rope over an abyss. Experiencing the tensions of twentieth-century life, many people have felt like tightrope walkers over a bottomless pit. To either side of them was Nothingness. Ahead of them was a vision of creative freedom and the development of human potentials. Often they were seized by vertigo and became unable to rivet their attention on the vision of hope. They fell into that bottomless pit, committing barbarous acts of torture and self-destruction on that descent. Nausea, the physical symptom of those possessed by Nothingness, continues to haunt the contemporary human condition. William Ernest Hocking has vividly described the terror of those torn apart by the conflicts and paradoxes of the twentieth century: "What we see is the moment-to-moment boundary of our being, the nothingness that completes itself in death, our own and that of the race: in such a world, riddled the while with horrorfilled actualities, how can a being aspiring and infinite be other than condemned to frustration?"[2]

Not everyone in the twentieth century, of course, has seen the situation as a tension between promise and peril. The perspective that guides this book has been held by many social thinkers, but not the majority. Its exponents have tended to be those sociologists and social philosophers who were concerned with the greater attainment of human freedom, the patterns of coercion and domination which restrict freedom in contemporary society, and the development of methods for studying social relations which take account of feeling, choice and mental image of the world, as well as behavior. Sociologists such as Erving Goffman, Georges Gurvitch, Pitirim Sorokin, Morris Ginsberg, C. Wright Mills, Radhakamal Mukerjee, E. T. Hiller, and Peter Berger, among others, fall into this tradition. Other perspectives have interpreted the twentieth century as a time of increasing progress towards a society in which people will be judged by their achievement of tasks rather than by their family, racial, and national origins, while other views have stressed the possibility or inevitability of a revolution which would abolish distinctions between social classes. These perspectives are optimistic about the future. Still other views have projected a decline of civilization and a relapse into barbarism. Both this pessimistic attitude and the optimistic viewpoints do not find ambivalence, paradox and uncertainty in the human condition, but identify clear trends. Often the way people think about society will be strongly influenced by such basic judgments of hope and despair.[3]

Among the most striking contrasts presented by the twentieth century is that between propaganda and science. The past several decades have seen the growing perfection of means to deceive people through the conscious manipulation of language and other media of communication. At the same time there has been an expansion of the use of scientific methods in the study of human action. Frequently the methods of science have been joined to the purpose of deceit, as when expert advisers to commercial and political elites determine just what distortions of the truth will best serve the interests of their employers.[4] The use of precise knowledge about human activity to deceive human beings has been, in part, responsible for the widespread feeling that human existence is bounded by Nothingness.[5] One of the factors that allows people to act in pursuit of their visions of hope is the presence of trust in human relations. When people begin to feel that they can no longer trust in the honesty of the messages communicated to them by their leaders, they lose confidence in the accuracy of their judgments about political and economic affairs. They believe that they cannot make intelligent decisions about public affairs, and withdraw to the restricted circle of private life where they can at least check their judgments by engaging in face-to-face relations.[6] Public life becomes a question mark to them, and it is a short step from a bare question mark to Nothingness. Responses to the "credibility gap" that marks contemporary life regardless of changes in leadership include impotent rage, cynicism, acceptance of the situation, apathy, continued faith that good men in power will set everything right, and serious attempts to understand the current human condition and the possibilities for its transformation.[7] This book is an attempt to contribute to understanding of the human condition in a world filled with propaganda, distortion, lies, and self-deception. The first step toward such understanding is a method of studying human existence.

THE METHOD OF SELF-UNDERSTANDING

How does an individual go about understanding the human condition? A satisfactory answer to this question can best be gained by trying to respond to another query, How does an individual go about understanding anything? Let us say that a person wanted to know how his automobile worked. It would be reasonable to direct someone with such a desire to a book about auto mechanics, a course on auto repair, or a person who knew how to fix cars and was willing to share his knowledge. After the person had learned the necessary background information, it would be wise to let him attempt to repair some automobiles himself. Through knowledge about automobiles gained through books, courses, or conversations, and knowledge by acquaintance with automobiles gained through fixing them, the individual would attain a fair understanding of how his automobile worked. Similarly, it appears that people go about understanding things by finding out what other people know about these things and directly acquainting themselves with them. Thus, understanding involves drawing upon previously acquired knowledge and testing this knowledge in particular cases. Through the test a person may meet unexpected situations, gain new knowledge and thereby add to the common stock of information about the thing.

Understanding the human condition is of course far more tricky than learning about how an automobile works. Understanding the human condition involves understanding people, and since the individual attempting to find out about human existence is a person himself, understanding the human condition includes self-understanding. Understanding the human condition is thus more complex: the individual who wants to learn about an automobile goes to others for the basic information that he needs, but the person who wants to understand the human condition must examine himself. In learning about automobiles there are good reasons for the individual to acquire knowledge about them before he gains knowledge by acquaintance with them. In understanding the human condition, the person is acquainted with it before he knows anything about it.[8] Thus, the method for understanding the human condition must be adapted to the task of self-understanding.

Figure 1.1. THE PROCESS OF SELF-UNDERSTANDING

Clarification:	Awareness of general beliefs about human existence
Generalization:	Identification of the intellectual tradition and social groups with which you share beliefs
Relativization:	Comparison of your beliefs with other traditions and groups
Commitment	Decision to attempt to realize a vision of human existence

The process of self-understanding involves four general phases—clarification, generalization, relativization, and commitment. In the phase of *clarification* the individual becomes aware of the general beliefs he holds about what is significant in human existence, and what is good and bad about it. In the phase of *generalization* the person discovers that he shares his beliefs with the members of certain present social groupings and is part of an historical tradition. In the phase of *relativization* the individual finds that other groupings and traditions hold some beliefs different from his own about the basic facts and central values of human existence. In the phase of *commitment* the person chooses a certain view of human existence as the basis for his action and makes it a living experiment. The following discussion will describe these phases in some detail.

CLARIFICATION

Consider the following question carefully. When you are not involved in any particular activity, when you are not attempting to satisfy any specific desire—when, in short, you are letting your mind roam free in thought—what do you think about? Many people experience great difficulty in answering a question like this. Frequently they say that they never let their thoughts roam free, and if they do, they never remember what passes through their minds. Other people experience no difficulty at all in responding. Some individuals say that they think about religion, and whether or not God exists. Others say that they think about how certain social changes might be accomplished. Still others say that they think about their future careers and what they might be able to accomplish in them. Still others relate fantasies that they conjure up in their minds.

The thoughts a person has when he lets his mind roam free are good indicators of what that individual considers important in the human condition. They are the basis from which the process of self-understanding begins. Bringing these thoughts clearly into awareness will provide the person with insight into his own vision of the human condition. For example, if a person says that when his mind roams free he thinks about how he can make large sums of money, it is likely that money is a central fact and value in his vision of the human condition. If he is asked why he thinks about money, he may answer with the cliché, "Money can't buy everything, but it sure helps." On further inspection it may turn out that this person believes that the good life consists in material luxury and independence from the commands of others. More careful examination may disclose that this individual believes that people are basically greedy and that they are in an endless rat race to acquire ever greater sums of money. At this point it can be said that the person has a fairly well developed vision of his view of the human condition. His central belief about human existence is that people are motivated to seek as much wealth as they can lay their hands on. His key values are luxury and independence.

Not everyone believes that money is the most important factor in human existence, although this belief is relatively popular in the United States.[9] There are many visions of the human condition, some of which conflict with one another. Some place freedom at the center of existence, some make one or another supposed instinct central, others focus attention on a particular activity like work, others believe that a relationship, like love, is most important, and still others orient existence around an idea of God. The phase of clarification involves bringing such beliefs into awareness so that the person can understand his general orientation to the human condition.

Once it has been described, the phase of clarification does not seem difficult to undertake. It appears to be far easier than attempting to understand how an automobile works. Yet many people stubbornly resist clarifying their beliefs about the human condition. This resistance need not be conscious, but may simply stem from a lack of exposure to multiple views. The reasons for this resistance help one to grasp the obstacles in the way of understanding the human condition.

Barriers to Clarification One of the most important reasons why people do not want to clarify their beliefs about the human condition is that they think that these beliefs may be stupid. Particularly among many people in the United States, there is fear of being judged ridiculous.[10] The twentieth century has been an age in which scientific knowledge has grown at a rapid rate. More and more areas of human

The Human Condition

experience have been turned over to specialists, and there has even been an effort to turn the mind over to experts. In addition to clergymen, who have always claimed to be specialists in the soul, there has been the growth of such professions as journalism, psychiatry, psychology, social work, advertising, public relations, and the various social sciences. The members of each of these professions view themselves, and are often viewed by others, as experts in the mind and its beliefs. Those who are intimidated by the experts in the mind are often afraid to examine their own beliefs. In order to understand the human condition, it is necessary to conquer this fear and to realize that one's mind is worthy of respect. Groups that hold economic and political power are quite satisfied to have people fear that they are stupid;[11] as long as such fear is widespread these groups have a better chance of getting their own way.

Related to the fear of being judged stupid is the fear that one will be judged insane. In some circles it is fashionable to brand as mentally ill people with whom one does not agree. People who take such insults to heart, or fear such insults will follow a declaration of beliefs, are likely to bury their beliefs about the human condition and forget about them. It is clear that the idea that one's beliefs about the human condition will indicate that one is mentally ill leads people to distrust their own judgments and makes it easier for elite groups to impose their definitions of experience on others.[12] This does not mean that the elite are responsible for the fears of being judged as stupid or mentally ill. Rather, such fears lessen the probability that critical self-examination will take place and thus leave the field open to imposed visions of the human condition. The best way to conquer the fear of being judged mentally ill is to carry through the entire process of self-understanding.

A third reason why people do not want to clarify their beliefs about the human condition is that they often think that beliefs are unimportant. One very frequently used cliché in the United States is that "talk is cheap." If talk is cheap, thoughts and beliefs are even cheaper. For many Americans, some vague notion of "action," "getting things done," or "doing something," is far more important than thinking.[13] A political system based on compromise between interest groups leads many people to hold that the reasons for acting are unimportant so long as decisions are made and the groups that scream the loudest get a larger piece of the pie.[14] Most advertising is based on the idea that as long as people buy the given product, and continue to buy it, the reasons for the purchases are unimportant.[15] The centrality of "selling" in American life has led people to the extreme notions that teachers are engaged in "selling" their subjects to students and that psychologists are engaged in "selling" interpretations of human existence to their patients.[16] The idea that beliefs are unimportant is itself a very important, and also a false, belief. It is important because it prevents people from examining their visions of the human condition. It is false because it makes a sharp separation between thought and action, when in fact thought and action are two inseparable phases of the same human process.[17]

The idea that beliefs are unimportant is based on the partial truth that much propaganda and advertising use ideas as a smokescreen to hide the pursuit of narrow interest. This partial truth ignores the wider truth that propaganda and advertising are themselves based on beliefs about the human condition. Some of these beliefs are that people are basically little children who crave pleasure, who attempt to avoid confronting unpleasant facts, who seek to blame their troubles on others, and who have a very short attention span.[18] Paradoxically, these beliefs appear to be true when large numbers of people act on the belief that ideas are unimportant. This discussion should show that there is no way of cutting off beliefs from action. The choice is not between whether one is a "thinker" or a "doer," but between whether one acts on beliefs that have been critically examined or on beliefs that are taken for granted without inspection.

There is another side to the idea that beliefs are unimportant. Many people use their beliefs about the human condition to "sell" themselves. The most pathetic way in which people make themselves into consumer goods is by adopting whatever beliefs about the human condition are current in the groups in which they want to gain acceptance. In this case, expressing certain beliefs is very important, but the truth of the beliefs is of little or no consideration. Those who use beliefs merely to gain acceptance are usually not interested in submitting their ideas about the human condition to critical self-examination. This is because they are ready to change their ideas as soon as it becomes fashionable to do so. Beneath, this chameleonlike existence, however, is a particular vision of the human condition, in which the most important factor in human life is making a favorable impression on people and being accepted as an insider.[19] For the person who uses beliefs to gain acceptance, existence is not so much a rat race in which people compete for wealth as a popularity contest without end. Perhaps the ultimate paradox in using beliefs to win popularity is the person who expresses the idea that one should strive for independent judgment in order to be accepted into a group of people who claim to cherish nonconformity.

There is an apparent contradiction in using beliefs merely to gain acceptance. If everyone acted merely to win popularity, each person would be trying to discover the widely held beliefs. However, there would be no source of beliefs about the human condition. Thus, people who use beliefs to gain acceptance depend for their ideas on people who are motivated by other considerations. In the United States, many of the beliefs adopted by those in the popularity rat race spring from business advertising and political propaganda, which are motivated by profit and power rather than by social acceptance. This means that the acceptance seekers are abdicating their judgment to the image makers of complex organizations.[20] They are content to trade their minds for a smile.

Using beliefs to gain acceptance is only a special case of using them for any number of ulterior purposes. Sometimes people who become aware of the techniques of advertising and propaganda reach the conclusion that, if so many of those highly placed in organizations resort to deception and distortion, they ought to get in on the action too. Everyone is familiar with the salesman who is willing to adopt racist attitudes when he believes that they will influence a purchase, but will become a staunch defender of human equality when this posture will help along a sale. Underlings will adopt the views of supervisors to speed their promotions, and politicians are notorious for changing their views of human nature in response to the polled opinions of the various groups in their constituencies. In many cases politicians conduct their own polls when running for office so that they can make their appeals effective. Those who simply manipulate beliefs for profit or power normally resist examining their visions of the human condition. Underlying their cynical use of ideas is the firm conviction that human life is a frantic scramble after power and privilege, and that only those willing to face up to the necessity of using force, fraud and bribery emerge the victors. It is apparent, however, that this view has a serious defect. If everybody was out to gain power and privilege, then nobody could be manipulated through an appeal to beliefs. Everyone would know that talk is cheap, and in that situation it would become so cheap as to be completely ineffective. This means that the success of people who manipulate beliefs for power and profit depends upon the existence of people who take ideas seriously and care about whether or not they are true. Hence, the manipulators invent a category of "suckers" who are mentally defective in the sense that they do not believe that the human condition is an endless rat race. Suckers are defined as subhumans who are soft-headed and woolly-minded enough to care whether or not their beliefs are true and their principles of action are right. While this is not the explicit view of all advertisers and propagandists, it has been the belief of many of them—for example, the promoter P. T. Barnum and the Nazi Joseph Goebbels.

One way of responding to advertising and propaganda is to make oneself into a manipulator of ideas. Many intelligent people reach the conclusion that truth is of little value in the contemporary world, and decide that if they are not going to be victims they will have to victimize others. A second way of responding to manipulation is the one which guides this book. This mode of response assumes that many current visions of the human condition, particularly those communicated by large organizations, are not offered in good faith. Given this situation, a person who believes everything that he reads and hears is a sucker. If an individual does not want to become an exploiter and also does not want to be a sucker, he must develop a way of understanding the human condition that will allow him to see through the various forms of propaganda and self-deception present in the contemporary world. The first step toward such understanding is clarification of one's own vision of the human condition.

Another reason why people do not want to clarify their beliefs about the human condition is that they think that beliefs are private matters. Taking this attitude into account, public opinion pollsters usually assure that their respondents will remain anonymous. In the United States a popular response when an individual's ideas are being questioned is, "I have a right to my own opinions." It is frequently difficult to determine just what this statement means. In most conversations where ideas are brought into question, there is no attempt by the critic to throw the other person into jail, do brain surgery on him, deprive him of a job, or ridicule him. Thus, the critic is not usually out to punish the other person for his ideas. He is not even trying to stop the other person from holding his ideas by any means other than discussion. Why, then, does the other individual assert a right to his own opinions?

The person being questioned appears to be saying that people have a right to their own opinions whether or not they are false or contradictory. This is presumably not a legal right to be enforced by the police and the courts. There are many reasons why it is desirable not to make the holding of false and contradictory beliefs illegal, including the tremendous expense that would be involved in enforcing such laws. Further, efficient mind-reading devices have not yet been invented; and finally it is frequently difficult to determine that a belief is false. Thus, when a person claims that he has a right to his own beliefs, he seems to be asserting a moral right. This often is seen essentially as a right not to engage in self-examination. Can such a right be defended?

The basis for the claim that one has a right not to engage in self-examination is that beliefs are a form of private property. Just as a person has a right to decorate his room with banana peels rather than paintings, regardless of canons of good taste, so, it is claimed, he also has a right to decorate his mind with any ideas that appeal to him, regardless of their truth or consistency. This might be a plausible claim if ideas were merely decorative property. However, if thought and action are closely linked together, and if basic ideas about the human condition are orientation points of the entire structure of a person's action, then basic beliefs about the human condition affect others besides the individual people who hold them.[21] These other people may have a legitimate interest in seeing that the individual's beliefs about the human condition do not result in harm to them. Further, it is difficult to determine in just what sense beliefs are private. Beliefs about the human condition can be put into words and communicated to others. Thus, they are not impenetrable "secrets" of the "mind." Beliefs about the human condition can be tested for their truth or falsity. Such beliefs are never the result of pure invention by the individual. How, then, are they private? The most that can be said is that beliefs about the human condition can be kept secret. Whether or not one has an absolute right to refrain from examining them is another question. The previous discussion shows that such a right is not self-evident.

The idea that beliefs are private matters and, therefore, need not be submitted to examination, is usually related to the fears of being judged stupid or insane and the use of beliefs to further ulterior purposes. This fear frequently goes beyond an unwillingness to clarify one's intimate personal concerns to a resistance to examining beliefs about public matters. It is a stock trick of propagandists to tell people that they can trust their own unexamined judgments, and that they do not have to take criticisms of their life-styles seriously. This trick is played when the propagandist has good reason to believe that widespread prejudices and attitudes are favorable to increasing the power and profit of his employers. When prejudices run against the interests of elite groups, propagandists will talk about the need for "leading public opinion," educating the public, and courageous leadership in the long-term interest in the face of short-sighted criticism. Hence, propagandists believe that people have a right to their opinions so long as those opinions support the interests of influential groups. One of the guiding themes of this book is that nobody has a right to his own opinions about the human condition if he is unwilling to undertake self-examination. This does not mean that we would like to send the police after those who do not examine themselves, or that we would like people to submit their beliefs about the human condition to a panel of sociologists for scrutiny and approval. Rather, we hold that because thought and action are so intimately related, nobody has the right to abdicate this judgment about human affairs and to make himself the unwitting tool of one or another pressure group. While this statement may appear to be harsh, we would rather be candid about our values than disguise them. It is partly for our own benefit that we urge you to examine your beliefs about the human condition. We would be far happier in a world where more people had respect for their minds. The fastest way to respect your mind is to get to know it. Also, it is important to remember that if you have any misgivings, nobody else has to know that you are questioning yourself.

The Comfort of Unquestioning Faith   Finally, people do not want to clarify their beliefs about the human condition because they believe that the opinions they hold are correct and are in no need of further definition. Many people think that, since their beliefs have served them fairly well for a number of years, there is no sense in taking the trouble to examine them and see what they really are. Others are convinced that they have some sort of "intuition" that allows them to make correct snap judgments about the situations they confront. For example, the promotion of myths about women's intuition may encourage females to renounce careful examination of their ideas. Still other people are content to follow some authority, such as a church, political party, or prestigious relative. They hold that this authority is far more likely to interpret the human condition correctly than they are. Other people have adopted a dogma, or a set of articles of faith, through which they interpret the human condition. They repeat the formulas of this dogma, whether it is based in a religious creed, a political program, an economic doctrine, or a theory of human nature, without understanding what they mean. Holding such a creed makes them appear to know what they are talking about, and they seem to have an answer to every question. However, when they are asked to define the meanings of their central terms and to account for inconsistencies in what they say, it becomes obvious that they usually are hopelessly confused. Their pat formulas have been concealing ill-formed and unclarified visions of the human condition. They have been using their dogmas as an excuse for avoiding self-examination—and even for avoiding any thinking at all.

Many people say, "I would really be happy if I could only have a faith and believe that all of my opinions were correct." There is no way of responding to this statement but to ask oneself whether one really would be happy in such a situation. There are some benefits to believing that all of one's ideas about the human condition are correct. First, there is a freedom from nagging doubts about what it is possible to expect from oneself and others. Once a person has settled on a particular vision of the human condition, his moral universe is structured, in the sense that he has figured out a way of apportioning rights and duties among people. He knows which actions are right and which ones are wrong, what things are good for human beings and what things are bad, when people are to be held responsible for their behavior and when they are not to be held accountable, and even, perhaps, in what the destiny of the human species consists. Freedom from doubt leads into the second benefit of certainty—i.e., confidence in action. People who have unquestioned faith in the correctness of a particular vision of the human condition often find it easier to take decisive action than do others.[22] When they are confronted with disputes they will unwaveringly support those who share their faith, even to the extent of making such statements as, "My country right or wrong." When they are confronted with problems, they will straightforwardly point out that these problems were caused by people who did not share their creed. They have a program for the future and are not faced with agonizing decisions about what actions will be most productive nor with wrenching second thoughts about whether they have accomplished anything.

The advantages of unexamined faith should be weighed against one central disadvantage. Once a person believes that the opinions he holds about the human condition are correct and are in no need of further definition, personal growth becomes very difficult for him.[23] Such a person has frozen himself at a particular place and time in history, and as events proceed he becomes more and more to look like an antique.[24] He becomes incapable of assimilating fresh experience and appreciating it for what it is. Everything new is twisted to look like a tired example of the old. Adaptation to significant changes is impeded and, even more important, it becomes difficult for the person to make a creative contribution to the continual task of reorganizing the human condition. The person who locks himself into a narrow set of beliefs which he refuses to examine, or even bring clearly into awareness, sacrifices his chances to appreciate the complexities and fresh experiences of the human condition.[25] He is the same today as he was yesterday, and he can look forward to a similar tomorrow. In cutting himself off from large chunks of experience, the person has gained a superficial and, ultimately, a false security. Since he will not understand others who do not share his beliefs, some of them will be able to take advantage of him. If his beliefs are inappropriate to changing circumstances he may bring himself to personal ruin. However, even if a set of rigid beliefs did not involve the risk of ruin, is the vision of being the same tomorrow as you are today and were yesterday really that appealing? Essentially, it is your answer to this question which will decide whether or not you will undertake the task of self-examination. If you conceive of the self as a process, continually encountering and organizing new experiences, you will welcome self-examination. If you conceive of the self as property, which can be stolen by greedy brain pickers and which must be protected by a veil of secrecy, you will shun self-examination. It is apparent that we are writing this book because we believe that the self is process, not property.[26] The idea that the self is property is behind most of the obstacles to clarifying one's orientation towards the human condition. It shows a profound disrespect for the creative capacities of the mind.

Figure 1.2. BARRIERS TO CLARIFICATION

People tend to avoid clarifying their images of human existence when:
1. They believe that their ideas may betray stupidity.
2. They believe that others may judge them to be mentally ill.
3. They use ideas merely to gain social acceptance.
4. They use ideas merely to gain such ulterior ends as power or profit.
5. They believe that ideas about human existence are private matters.
6. They believe that ideas are private property to be used as the "owner" sees fit.
7. They believe that their ideas are absolutely correct.

Do you confront any of these barriers? If so, are you willing to overcome them?

GENERALIZATION

Clarification was discussed at such great length because it is the single most important step in the process of self-examination. Once people have enough interest in their thoughts about the human condition to subject them to scrutiny, the obstacles in the way of completing the process are relatively minor. Yet even though clarification of one's basic beliefs about the human condition is the most decisive step that one takes on the road to self-understanding, it is merely a beginning. The next step, generalization, takes the person outside of himself.

Once a person has clarified what he considers to be significant and valuable in the human condition, he is prepared to begin the search for the tradition of which he is a representative. Finding the tradition of thought that one's ideas about the human condition represent is the essential feature of the phase of generalization. There are two aspects of the search, both of which are integral to self-examination. First, there is an attempt to identify the present social groupings whose ideas are closest to one's own. Second, there is an effort to trace the historical development of one's beliefs. The key to the process of generalization is that the person situates himself in a social and cultural field, rather than conceiving of himself as a detached and isolated individual.

The process of generalization is based on a particular way of looking at human existence which follows from the idea that the self is a process. According to some people, human beings are born into the world with a fixed nature from which they cannot deviate.[27] Such people view the self as a thing with certain properties: a kind of machine. Once there is knowledge about how the machine works, it is possible to use the machine for one's own purposes. For example, if one is sure that human beings are "naturally" greedy, one will attempt to play upon greed to gain one's purposes. Other motivations, such as curiosity and desire for love, will be ignored. As another example, suppose that a person believes that human beings will do what brings them rewards and shun what brings them punishments. In order to gain his purposes, such a person will attempt to manipulate rewards and punishments rather than appeal to the independent judgment of human beings.

Pitfalls of Depersonification There are several criticisms of viewing the self as a thing. First, once a person has adopted a fixed view of human nature, he is forced to explain away all evidence to the contrary. For example, the person who believes that human beings are naturally greedy must explain away acts that are apparently motivated by such impulses as curiosity or love. There are two ways in which this is normally done. First, the person argues that the curiosity or love merely hides conscious or unconscious greed. Once the greed has been made unconscious it becomes virtually useless as a way of understanding human activity. Second, the person argues that curiosity and love are merely forms of greed, because people enjoy satisfying their curiosity and engaging in relations of love. If it is pointed out that many lovers undergo pain to aid their loved ones, the person responds that they still "like love better," or else they would never have suffered the pain. This kind of argument convinces many people that human beings really are motivated by greed. However, a close look at it reveals that it proves almost nothing. To say that people are greedy because they do what they prefer to do is to define greed as acting on one's preferences, regardless of what they are. There is no law against defining greed in this way, but it deprives the term of almost all its ordinary meaning and force. Also, there is a problem in the idea of preferences. How does one find out about someone's preferences? It seems that this discovery can only be made by seeing what the person does. Thus, there are no preferences apart from actions. This means that all actions are being defined as greedy simply because they are actions. Again, there is no law against using the word greed as a synonym for the word action. It is appropriate, though, to ask whether this is really what the defender of the greed theory originally intended to say.

The second defect in viewing the self as a thing is that it tears the human condition out of history. For those who believe in a fixed human nature, the human condition always remains essentially the same. For example, those who believe that human nature is greedy often hold that politics has always been and always will be a form of highway robbery.[28] For them, it does not matter who controls the state; the rulers will always be trying their hardest to extort the last pound of flesh out of the ruled. Cases of political corruption, crime, and espionage (for example, the Watergate affair) tend to give support for this view. Frequently, they draw the lesson from this argument that concerted and collective action to promote social change is foolhardy, and that the only sensible strategies for the individual are to get a piece of the action or to withdraw from the battle into private consumption, drugs, or a "home in the heart of the country." Paradoxically, the ruling elite thrive on such cynicism as long as they do not have to mobilize the population for great sacrifices. Cynicism, bred by fixed theories of human nature, at least keeps people out of the opposition.

Tearing the human condition out of history deprives people of clear knowledge of their concrete historical possibilities. Every situation in which people find themselves provides some opportunities and closes off others. For example, most university classrooms, built with fixed seats all pointing in the same direction, make lecturing by the professor easy and open discussion difficult. Rigid views of human nature are entirely irrelevant to analyzing such concrete opportunities. Simply stating that human beings are greedy will not account for why university classrooms are arranged with lecturing rather than discussion in mind. Such a statement also will not provide any help in understanding how it might be possible to provide spaces for learning and inquiry which would encourage discussion. Similarly, the five-subject undergraduate schedule provides opportunities for information about a variety of experiences, but little chance for in-depth study of any experience. Fixed theories of human nature will be of no help in analyzing this situation either. The general ideas that do help in understanding such situations are those clustering around the view of the self as a process with multiple possibilities for development at each historical juncture.

The phase of generalization, or searching for the social groupings and historical traditions that one represents, is only possible because the self is a process organizing meanings and relations. Human beings act on visions of the future (projects), which involve human creations (cultural objects) and other people (relations).[29] If each human being was a completely unique and self-contained individual, there would be no possibility for generalization. It is only because the person learns about possible meanings of the human condition *from* others and can communicate them *to* others that visions of the human condition come to be shared by people over time. Thus, the idea that human beings are naturally greedy is historically specific. It was created by particular human beings at a particular time, has been held more by some groups than by others, and has served a variety of specific purposes. It is an idea most widely held where private business is important, because many business methods play upon the motivation of greed. Where business methods are not very important the idea is not likely to become dominant.[30]

The phase of generalization can be defined best through an example. There are a number of people in the United States who believe that the social group, rather than the individual, is the most important source of creative ideas, that the ultimate need of human beings is belongingness and group membership, and that there are systematic methods available through which people can be engineered into belongingness.[31] Taken together, these beliefs form a powerful and sometimes compelling vision of the human condition. The vision is compelling because many innovations and new developments appear to emerge anonymously out of vast organizations, composed of endless agencies and committees, and because many human beings seem to be lost and in search of belongingness.[32] The vision is powerful because large organizations frequently try to control the kinds of human relations that occur within them, and the kinds of personalities that develop out of these relations.

Suppose that, after clarifying his vision of the human condition, a person discovered that he held the beliefs listed above. If he wanted to proceed to the phase of generalization he would ask, "Who else holds these ideas and where did they come from?" He would find out that these ideas are current among many people who work in the middle levels of large organizations and who are given little opportunity for independent initiatives. He would also find out that these ideas began to become widespread after World War I, when the image of the self-made man was tarnished by contact with the realities of vast organizations. These organizations required people who would cooperate with their co-workers rather than compete with them, and in order to help meet this requirement a literature developed on ways of engineering consent. William H. Whyte, Jr., in *The Organization Man* did an extensive study of this vision of the human condition and summarized its claims: "Man exists as a unit of society. Of himself, he is isolated, meaningless; only as he collaborates with others does he become worthwhile, for by sublimating himself in the group, he helps produce a whole that is greater than the sum of its parts."[33] Whyte also identified the groups of middle managers who hold these beliefs and showed how they grew out of tendencies in American philosophy which emphasize the importance of human relations over human creations and personal choices. Through his work, Whyte was able to generalize the central beliefs about the human condition held by many Americans.

It is important to note that a person willing to exercise his imagination and listen closely to what is said around him could go quite deeply into the phase of generalization without reading books such as Whyte's. A person holding the middle manager's creed could try to remember where he picked it up and try to figure out whose purposes it might serve. Once he had made some judgments about these matters he could seek out books that would tell him the history of these ideas and how they had developed over time. Through generalization the person would be able to situate himself historically. He would find out which groupings shared his ideas about the human condition and what kind of world these groupings were trying to create. Generalization, then, makes the process of self-examination social rather than individual. The person is no longer locked up inside of himself with private and arbitrary judgments and feelings. He shares his problems, interpretations, and programs with others. He has, in the terms of C. Wright Mills, made his private problems public.[34]

Obstacles to Generalization Just as there were obstacles to clarifying one's basic ideas about the human condition, so there are obstacles to undertaking the phase of generalization. The most important barrier to generalization is the desire that one's beliefs be unique. Many people in the United States believe that it is a virtue to be unique, and become upset whenever they realize that they have a great deal in common with others.[35] They refuse to look for social groupings expressing ideas similar to their own, because they feel that they are less human if they are representatives of a tradition.[36] This attitude demands careful examination.

The most obvious defect in the attitude is that, whether or not one wants to admit it, most of his beliefs have a long past and are widespread among one or more present social groupings. Thus, when a person refuses to generalize his beliefs on the grounds that he is unique, he is not stating a fact, but merely burying his head in the sand. Further, it is appropriate to ask whether or not beliefs about the human condition serve any purpose if they are unique. A central belief about the human condition is a statement that claims to be true about the human condition in general. If such a statement is unique to an individual and that individual claims it is true, it means that he also claims that others are living in falsehood. He then must ask himself whether he values his uniqueness more than he values others believing the truth. He may also ask himself how it happened that he alone has been able to perceive the truth about the human condition.

The preceding discussion was intended to open the possibility that beliefs about the human condition are not the kinds of things that one would want to make a mark of one's uniqueness. Every human being is at least unique in the sense that no two human beings have been through exactly the same experiences, and no two human beings share exactly the same position in space-time. Individuality and uniqueness can be emphasized through differences in taste and the organization of life-style. Such differences lead to the expansion of human appreciation. However, seeking uniqueness through beliefs seems to be a misplaced use of beliefs, which are claims that certain judgments are true. If a person argues that his ideas about the human condition are true for him, but not for others, he is either saying that his judgments are based on a limited slice of experience (a sensible statement) or that everybody is completely different (a questionable judgment). The wish that one's beliefs be unique is an outcome of the idea that the self is private property and that beliefs are a part of that property. It is similar to the desire of many women not to wear the same outfit to a party as someone else.

The desire for unique beliefs has two social consequences. First, it prevents people from recognizing their allies in social struggles and thereby furthers the spread of dispersed masses of floating individuals.[37] Second, it is useful to ruling elite groups because it prevents the formation of oppositions. It is merely another way in which people are tricked out of using their minds.

Related to the desire for unique beliefs is the desire for originality. The worship of originality is only a specialized form of the worship of uniqueness. Often when people clarify their beliefs about the human condition they experience a joy in self-understanding and, since they have never seen themselves so clearly before, think that they have far surpassed what others have been able to learn. Sometimes they experience a letdown when they find that many people in the past have shared their beliefs about the human condition and have expressed these beliefs with great precision. Sometimes those who desire originality more than understanding will attempt to prove that their ideas really are completely new and bear only superficial resemblance to the beliefs of the past and present. Perhaps what is saddest is that some people who have overcome the fear of being labeled stupid, and have clarified their beliefs, come to think of themselves as stupid when they learn that their ideas are not original. This misplaced judgment shows that many people are at least as embarrassed and misinformed about their minds as they are about their sexual relations and their capabilities for violence.

Placing originality above understanding has the same consequences as placing uniqueness above truth. The most important consequence is to impede the growth of solidarity among human beings. There are some great benefits to solidarity. First, generalization allows one to learn about one's own thoughts from people who have spent time and effort trying to work out their implications. Someone who believes that the emphasis on group creativity of the middle managers works against human dignity can learn a great deal from Whyte's attacks on the ethic of belongingness. Second, generalization helps a person find out who his allies are in current social struggles. If thought and action are related, generalization adds a new significance and importance to one's action. Third, and most important, generalization provides what can best be called intellectual friendships. The person finds out that he is not a lonely thinker, crying in a wilderness. There are others who have shared important parts of his vision, even if it is possible that nobody else's vision has been exactly the same.[38] Originality and uniqueness may have some snob appeal and romantic glamour, but in the long run they leave a person alienated and alone. This does not mean that people should seek "belongingness" for its own sake. Rather, it means that people should not avoid finding out just how far their beliefs about the human condition extend in time and space. At this point, we cannot resist firing a parting shot at those who resist generalization. How many people get upset when they realize that their belief that the earth is round is not unique to them? How many people are uncomfortable that their discovery that two plus two equals four is not original? Why, then, do some people care whether or not their visions of the human condition are unique and original? We believe that it has something to do with the widespread idea that a person's life is his private property.

Figure 1.3 BARRIERS TO GENERALIZATION

People tend to avoid generalizing their images of human existence when:
1. They would like to believe that their beliefs are unique.
2. They would like their beliefs to be original.

Do you value uniqueness over truth and originality over understanding?

RELATIVIZATION

The person who generalizes learns that there are people who share his central beliefs about the human condition. However, at the very moment that one becomes conscious of his intellectual friends, one is also made aware of those who disagree with him, and of their ideas. Recognition—and, hopefully, appreciation—of intellectual opponents goes along with acquiring intellectual friends.

The next step after the phase of generalization in the process of self-examination is the phase that has come to be known by the cumbersome word *relativization.* Through relativizing his beliefs about the human condition, the person becomes conscious that his view of human existence is merely one among many visions, and that sincere and intelligent people have fundamental differences with him. He also learns about the structure and content of some of these other beliefs and comes to appreciate why others would hold them. He discovers that different beliefs about the human condition are associated with different social groupings and represent long historical traditions.[39]

Aspirations of Different Groups The phase of relativization can be understood through an illustration of how it might occur in a specific case. Suppose a person discovers that he holds the middle manager's vision of human existence, and that he believes that the fundamental motivation of human beings is to seek "belongingness." This person has clarified and generalized his beliefs. However, in the process of clarifying and generalizing he has found out about other visions of the human condition. He has discovered that, for certain specialists and higher managers in organizations, the fundamental drive of human beings is for interesting work to which they can make a personal and creative contribution. For these people, belongingness is far less valued than autonomy and individual initiative. Further, he comes to realize that most of the clerical and production force in the organization is interested primarily neither in belongingness nor creative initiative, but in security. These people view the human condition primarily in terms of the social life-cycle of birth, marriage, child rearing, and/or breadwinning, leisure, and death. They believe that human beings are motivated to acquire the "good things in life," among which are security of income, a happy family life, a decent neighborhood to live in, and some of the comforts and diversions provided by consumer goods. Finally, he becomes acutely aware of the poor and of the members of minority groups who consider themselves dispossessed by the other social groupings, and who believe that human existence is a power struggle between dominant and subordinate groups. For them, the fundamental human drive is for self-determination, in the sense of economic independence, political freedom, control over the content of education and determination over the style of living that will characterize their communities. Through relativization, the person who arrives at an understanding of these diverse groups has performed a revolution perhaps greater in its impact than the one performed by Copernicus when he argued that the earth was not at the center of the universe. The person who relativizes is no longer at the center of the social universe. He merely represents one stream of thought and one mode of action among many.

As the person becomes aware of the different images of the human condition held by the members of different social groupings, he grasps how closely related these visions are to the activities that people perform.[40] The middle manager and technician must work in a group setting. They do not make policies, but are given directives from above. Thus, their main problem is to cooperate efficiently to fulfill plans programmed by others. A vision of group creativity, a drive to belongingness and the systematic adjustment of human efforts fits very well with this kind of work. The upper-professional higher manager, however, does make policy, and is continually confronted with new challenges from the competition of other organizations and the demands of more specialized groups at lower echelons. For him, a vision of human existence stressing creative initiative is more appropriate than one emphasizing belongingness. Similarly, belongingness is not a primary factor in the work of most clerical and production personnel, because their tasks center around operating machines or engaging in standardized interpersonal relations (e.g., checking groceries in a supermarket), rather than in coordinating group efforts toward programmed goals. Their satisfactions lie mainly outside of their jobs and, therefore, their visions of the human condition stress family and leisure life. Finally, while the dispossessed emphasize group solidarity, they are not chiefly concerned with belongingness. They are on the outside of the major organizations, and are demanding greater rights and a greater share of the social product. They have the least secure and most menial work, and relatively high proportions of their members are unemployed. Thus, the vision of human existence as a power struggle fits their situation well. Rather than belongingness, they want respect, and the rights that go along with it.

Relativization gives a person a more accurate understanding of the human condition and of his place in it, a firmer grounding for his action with respect to others and a deeper appreciation for different kinds of people. Understanding is furthered by recognition of the partiality of one's own vision and the cogency of other visions. Action is more intelligent because one knows better what to expect from members of other groups and how one's communications will be received by members of these groups. Appreciation is aided by imaginatively living through the visions of other people. While the phase of relativization provides all these benefits, there are obstacles that people confront in undertaking it. As with the other phases, the barriers to relativization are tied up with the image of the self as property.

Barriers to Relativization The most important obstacle to relativization is the fear that seriously considering other beliefs about the human condition will disclose that one's own ideas are trivial. There are two varieties of this fear. First, there is anxiety that one will find that he has been a dupe and a fool for most of his life. While this hardly ever proves to be the case, because most widespread visions of the human condition have compelling features, there is serious question about whether a person really wants to keep himself in the dark about other ideas simply to preserve a false sense of certainty. Refusing to relativize one's beliefs is one of the greatest inhibitors to personal growth. Second, there is the anxiety that relativization leads to making all beliefs about the human condition trivial. There is an idea that just because honest and intelligent people hold different, and frequently clashing, visions of the human condition, all such visions are equally true or equally false. This means that beliefs about the human condition become merely matters of arbitrary personal preference.[41]

It should be clear that this kind of corrosive attitude does not necessarily follow from the process of relativization. First, the idea that all central beliefs about the human condition are equally true or equally false often stems from confusing honesty and intelligence with truth. Just because a person is sincere and bright does not mean that he is correct. The truth of a proposition is determined by testing it against experience, not by the sincerity with which it is held. Second, many differences between visions of the human condition are based on the slices of experience to which the people who hold them have access. The differences between the beliefs of the middle manager and the dispossessed person are in great part a result of the different experiences they have undergone. The middle manager does not confront discrimination and prejudice every day. The dispossessed person does not spend much of his life coordinating complex activities in accordance with organizational plans. The ideas about the human condition current in the various groupings are not so much falsehoods as distortions of the whole stemming from partial experience of the whole and manipulations of ideas by elite groups. Basic ideas about the human condition arise out of people taking the most central experiences of their own lives and projecting them onto the whole of human existence.[42] This process of distortion is speeded along by packaged interpretations of the human condition communicated to specific groups by advertisers and propagandists. The only way to prevent one's partial truths from becoming monstrous falsehoods is through undertaking the process of relativization.

A second obstacle to relativization is the comfort that some people feel with their beliefs and their unwillingngess to suffer the pains of questioning them. It is pleasant to feel that the world is in order, that one is at the center of the social universe, and that one's own tradition is the only one worth understanding. However, the same objections apply both to the person who is unwilling to relativize his beliefs because he is comfortable with them and to the person who is unwilling to clarify his beliefs because he thinks he has a "right" to them. It is appropriate to select a bed with an eye to whether it will be comfortable, but since beliefs and activities are so closely linked, comfort may not be the proper criterion for determining whether or not beliefs should be held. Placing comfort ahead of truth is very closely linked with the idea that the self is private property. People often hold on to consumer goods or get rid of them on the basis of the pleasure or pain that they derive from them. The goods are their property to dispose of as they wish. When the idea of property dominates the self, even beliefs are made into consumer goods.

Distortions Brought about by the Communication-Gap Theory A third obstacle to relativization is the idea that all differences in basic beliefs about the human condition stem from communication gaps. The person possessed by this idea believes that there is only one "reasonable" way of viewing the human condition (his own), and that every sincere and "normal" person shares his vision.[43] He is convinced there are no fundamental disagreements among honest human beings, and apparent conflict is a result of misunderstandings rather than clashing interests or contradictory premises. Since there is only one "reasonable" way of viewing the human condition, there is no reason to relativize one's beliefs. All that needs to be done is to translate what others are saying into one's own frame of reference.

The idea that all disagreements over human destiny stem from communication gaps is simply false. However, it is very widespread in the United States today, particularly in large organizations. Accepting his organization's propaganda as the only normal way of looking at the world, the middle manager will tell the workers that management is trying to look out for the workers' interests, and will tell the dispossessed that they really crave belongingness rather than self-determination.[44] The idea that all disagreements result from communication gaps is extremely useful to the elite. It allows them to twist the demands of dispossessed groups for power into demands for equal opportunity within the system. It allows them to say that "violence will accomplish nothing; come let us reason together." Of course, those who already have power can afford to spend their time "reasoning" for as long as it takes to wear down the opposition. Further, the communications media can be blamed for creating passions and divisions, and the responsibility of leadership can be avoided. Finally, the communication-gap theory allows elite groups to play on "good intentions" rather than performance. They can try to convince people that they are "trying as hard as humanly possible" to right all the wrongs. This seems to mean that as long as they are "trying" it does not matter a bit what they accomplish.

The communication-gap theory lulls a great many people into complacency. It allows them to say such things as: "We're all basically the same, aren't we? Why can't we start talking about some of the good things about the country, rather than trying to tear it down all the time? After all, the minorities just want a little more of the pie. If people only used a little common sense they'd see that we have a good country and that we're trying hard to give everyone a fair shake. It's just that you can't change everything overnight." Such people would be quite disturbed if they became acutely aware that there are blacks in the United

States who want to bake their own pie and who do not see themselves as basically the same as whites.[45] Thus, the communication-gap theory is another way in which people bury their heads in the sand (or in the pie). It is simply the most sophisticated of the myths that keep people from self-examination, and is to be avoided like the plague by anyone out to seek truth. The communication-gap theory also has another disagreeable feature. It is quite conceited to believe that one's own view of the human condition is the only "reasonable" one and that no "normal" person would hold any other. This is making disagreement a form of mental illness.[46] It is quite useful for the elite to spread the rumor that the opposition is mentally ill. Relativization increases understanding, effectiveness in action, and appreciation. Its only drawback is that it decreases conceit.

Figure 1.4. BARRIERS TO RELATIVIZATION

People tend to avoid relativizing their images of human existence when:
1. They are afraid that confrontation with new beliefs will show them that they have been fools and dupes.
2. They are afraid that they will find all beliefs to be trivial.
3. They feel comfortable with their present beliefs.
4. They believe that all differences of opinion about human existence are a result of communications gaps.

Do you avoid discussions about politics and religion? If so, why?

COMMITMENT

The final phase of the process of self-examination is commitment, or the development of a conscious view of the human condition and a plan of action based upon it. In clarification, one becomes aware of one's vision of the human condition and principles of action. In generalization, one discovers the roots of that vision in space and time. In relativization, one comes to understand and appreciate other basic beliefs about the human condition. In commitment, one uses the knowledge and appreciation one has gained about the human condition to devise a more adequate vision and to act in terms of it. This does not mean that increased understanding will always lead to altered action. There are barriers to commitment. However, if one has clarified, generalized, and relativized, he will at least be aware of whether he is acting on his explicit vision or on some implicit one—or, worst of all, on one forced upon him.

The phase of commitment is based on the insight that one is always acting in terms of some view of the human condition, whether or not one is fully aware of that vision. In the light of this, human freedom resides in becoming aware of alternative perspectives, and consciously choosing to act on one of them or to create a new vision out of the given material and whatever fresh insights are available. It is important to note that the phase of commitment does not necessarily come to a definite end, and that it contains all of the other phases within it. Each new situation presents a human being with fresh experience and new opportunities for extending awareness. In order to continue the process of self-examination, this experience must be clarified, generalized, relativized, and then judged with respect to its bearing on action. The phase of commitment means that human existence is a continual living experiment in which visions of the human condition are tested for their factual accuracy, logical consistency, comprehensiveness, felt quality, and fruitfulness for future action. These visions are tested not in some laboratory set apart from social life, but in the concrete human relations that take place from day to day. Each day that people try to solve their problems by assuming that human beings crave belongingness and that all disagreements stem from communication gaps, these assumptions are being tested. Each day that people go to work assuming that human nature is greedy and that good sense means getting in on the action, these assumptions are being tested. Of course, the tests are always incomplete, because it never happens that everybody is testing the same assumptions. This means that the results are never completely decisive, and that it is almost impossible to dislodge completely any widespread vision of the human condition. Further, the tests are self-certifying, because, for example, if everybody acted on the assumption that human nature is greedy, everybody would be greedy.[47] Theories of human nature are realized when people act on them. This is why the phase of commitment is so important. By acting on a vision of the human condition, one helps make that vision come true.

The incompleteness and self-certifying character of basic beliefs about the human condition are keys to why we consider the process of self-examination to be so important. If people merely take their visions of the human condition for granted they are actively creating a world which they do not even understand. Usually their unexamined beliefs help serve the interests of one or another elite group. Sometimes these beliefs, if fully carried out, would result in consequences that the holder of the beliefs would deplore. Imagine a world in which everybody was greedy, or a world in which everybody was passionately seeking belongingness. Most important, without conscious commitment undertaken after the other phases of self-examination, a person cannot have respect for his mind. Lacking such respect, an individual easily becomes the pawn of others, who most likely do not have his interests at heart. We, at least, find it very difficult to respect people who are unwilling to undertake self-examination, because we know that such people refuse to take responsibility for their lives. While this again may appear to be a harsh judgment, we make it because at one time we avoided self-inspection, and can remember what we were like at that time. We are aware of the obstacles to self-examination, not because we have engaged in laboratory experiments with human guinea pigs, but because we encountered these obstacles ourselves. Particularly difficult are some of the barriers standing in the way of passing from relativization to commitment.

Problems in Attaining Commitment The first obstacle to entering the phase of commitment is the idea that all central beliefs about the human condition are trivial. This idea, which has been discussed under the topic of relativization, appears in a slightly different context here. Sometimes the idea that visions of the human condition are trivial turns into the belief that the human condition itself is trivial or absurd.[48] This is not a difficult transition to make, especially in the light of the fact that visions are an integral component of human existence.

Frequently the person who believes that the human condition is trivial holds that life is merely a game, or that it does not matter what he does. Sometimes this is a convenient way of avoiding responsibility for one's actions. When questioned about some harmful action, an individual can say, "What does it matter since life is absurd anyway?" At other times the belief is a cry of regret for an absolute authority and a certainty which has been lost forever. At still other times it is a cry of despair from people who have been pushed into a corner and only have the narrowest of choices. There are times when an individual has a choice between doing something utterly repulsive or committing suicide. In such situations existence does seem absurd.

The idea that human existence is trivial or absurd is itself a vision of the human condition that can be judged against other visions. If a person acts in terms of it, she has made a commitment. As she lives out her experiment, she can judge whether or not she really finds life trivial. Perhaps there are some experiences that she particularly values over others. Perhaps she seeks these experiences and plans the rest of her life around them. For example, she may find happiness when she is alone in the woods or when she is making love or when she is eating a good meal. She may forget about the triviality of life when having these experiences. If she recognizes that she is taking something seriously, she is beyond the framework of triviality. She may still hold the belief that there is no ultimate meaning to human existence that can be determined by human beings, and she may feel pangs of regret about this, and even get periodically dizzy from looking into the abyss. However, she will also live for those experiences that seem valuable in themselves. If, on the other hand, she continues to find existence trivial, she will be stuck with that judgment and the actions that go along with it. In either case, she will have made a commitment and performed a living experiment.

A second obstacle to commitment is the fear of closing one's options. Many people who have gone as far as relativization view existence as a set of pure possibilities. They do not want to experiment with any particular possibility because this will prevent them from having other experiences. Thus, they remain in limbo, afraid of living out a particular life.[49] It is clear, however, that remaining in limbo is itself a particular kind of life with its own specific experiences of suspense, vacancy and always being on the edge of things but never fully participating. The person who fears closing his options has effectively closed them anyway.

There is no way of having one's cake and eating it too. Each person is always in a particular situation doing specific things.[50] There is, however, a way of preventing narrowness in one's life. This is by continually going through the process of self-examination, particularly the phase of relativization, and incorporating into one's commitment the valuable experiences that one discovers. For example, by observing the social protests of blacks and trying to understand the experience of dispossessed peoples, many whites added a new experience of militant social action to their lives. Such opportunities for incorporating new experience and acting on it are readily available in the complex world of today.

The final obstacle to commitment is the fear that one's actions will reveal one to be a fool. Here we return to the very beginning of the discussion, and to the major themes that we have emphasized. Too many people in the contemporary world lack confidence in their own minds. They are told that they should turn their thinking over to experts, that they cannot make their own decisions, that the world is too complex for them to understand. They are afraid to examine their own beliefs because they think that these beliefs are probably worthless anyway. They are afraid to commit themselves to living experiments because there are experts who supposedly know much more about human existence than they do. The purpose of this book is to combat these attitudes by showing that it is possible to increase your awareness of the human condition, and to provide you with a method for continually reconstructing your beliefs about human existence. It is our purpose to show you that you are not a fool, but that you are instead a representative of a long historical tradition with capacities for altering that tradition. With this end in mind, the next chapter will summarize the history of social thought. In reading that chapter try to separate your intellectual friends from your intellectual opponents. Through that process you will be generalizing and relativizing, and on your way to making a conscious commitment.

Figure 1.5. BARRIERS TO COMMITMENT

People tend to avoid making commitments when:
1. They think that all beliefs are trivial.
2. They believe that the human condition is absurd.
3. They would like to keep their options perpetually open.
4. They think that they may appear foolish to others.

Do you like to exist above life?

2
A BRIEF GUIDE TO SOCIAL THOUGHT

How does a person begin to understand the human condition and his projects within it? If an individual simply went to the library and began paging through books in the sociology section with the intent of clarifying and generalizing his ideas about human relations, he would probably meet with frustration. He would be confronted by a bewildering array of books and articles, directed to a wide variety of questions and containing different and often clashing answers to these questions. It would be possible for him to spend several years reading some of these books and articles at random. Through this experience he would slowly create an overall framework in which the various kinds of social thought made sense. He would have a map which would enable him to locate the various types of social thought as he encountered them, and to see how they related to his ideas about the human condition. It is the purpose of this chapter to try to save an individual concerned with understanding the human condition some time in identifying where he stands with respect to the history of social thought. This chapter, then, presents the broad outlines of a map of social thought. As you read through this chapter try to figure out which kinds of social thought you most agree with and then, if you have the time, read some of the authors with whom this type of thought is identified. This will allow you to clarify and generalize your image of the human condition. If you do not agree with any of the ideas discussed in the following pages, pick out the ideas that you disagree with most, read the authors who have expressed them and try to figure out why you disagree with them. This procedure will be just as useful in the process of self-understanding as the one stressing your agreement with a type of social thought.

There are many maps of social thought.[1] Some of them divide thought about the human condition according to place or time. Thus, there are books on German sociology, American social thought, Oriental social philosophy, and so on. Similarly, there are books on nineteenth-century sociology, twentieth-century sociology, and so on. Other maps divide social thought according to different answers to a central question. This is the approach taken here. The central question which will guide the following discussion is, What fundamental assumptions about the human condition have characterized social thought? Philip S. Haring has called such assumptions "grand conceptions by which I make sense of reality."[2] He argues that, whether or not a person realizes it, he is using such a grand conception to interpret the human condition. The task of the social thinker is to bring these conceptions clearly into awareness so that human beings can make conscious choices among the various frameworks through which human existence can be interpreted.

THE TYPES OF SOCIAL THOUGHT

There are four general ways in which the human condition can be interpreted, each one of which has many adherents in the contemporary world. The first grand conception is the *natural-law model.* This type of thinking, which appeared in the ancient civilizations of Greece, the Middle East, India and China, and was carried through in the Middle Ages, views the human being as an integral part of an orderly universe. According to this view, human beings are regulated by a moral law which they can grasp through divine revelation or reason, but which they are not free to change. Therefore, natural-law thinkers believe that there is a proper order to human existence, and that even if human beings do not always conform to that order, they are still ethically bound by it. The aim of natural-law thinkers has traditionally been to criticize the social life around them when it has not measured up to the moral standards they hold, and to describe the kinds of human relations that would measure up to these standards. If this discussion seems to be difficult to grasp, it is well to remember that most religious people hold some conception of natural law. For example, many Christians believe that the commandment to love thy neighbor as thyself is a natural law which people may break in many cases, but which they cannot change because it has been instituted by God.

The second general way in which the human condition can be interpreted is in some type of *monistic* or *one-factor model*. Those who hold the monistic model believe that the human condition should be interpreted in terms of a single organizing factor. According to this view, the activities of human beings can be understood in terms of the working of certain key forces that operate under one overriding concept. For example, some people believe that human beings have a primary drive to seek power over others. Whatever events occur in human relations, these people attempt to relate them to the power drive. Besides clear relations of domination, in which power is obviously involved, such relations as love are interpreted as concealed attempts to impose one's will on the other.[3] There are almost as many monistic theories of the human condition as there are human motivations and activities. Some monists hold that economic factors are primary (Marxism), others stress relations between the sexes (Freudianism), others racial factors (Lothrop Stoddard), and still others climate (Montesquieu). A person is likely to be a monist if he can give a precise answer to the question, What is human nature? Such a person frequently reduces human activity to some factor like greed, lust for power, desire for love, desire for approval, or the urge to survive biologically. Whatever factor is picked out, it is likely that there is a past or present thinker who has interpreted the human condition in its terms.

The third grand conception of the human condition is the *pluralistic model*. Those who hold some type of pluralistic model believe that there are a multiplicity of factors involved in the human condition, and that it is necessary to take account of all of these for a complete understanding of human existence. Pluralists tend to believe that each individual or each group is a unique combination of factors that will never be repeated again. Frequently they believe that the human condition is divided up into sectors such as the economic, political, social and cultural, each of which is relatively separate from the others, and each of which is studied by a special science (economics, political science, sociology, and anthropology). Both pluralism and monism are responses to the decline of natural law. Natural-law theorists are primarily concerned with discovering and applying the moral laws that people should follow if they are to lead the good or righteous life. Monists and pluralists, who frequently believe that there are no such discoverable laws, are far more interested in discovering and applying the factors they think determine human behavior.

The fourth grand conception of the human condition is the *process model*. This is the model held by the authors of this book. Those who hold the process model believe that events in the human condition can be best understood by organizing them around a single human process in which people continuously create and re-create the conditions under which they live. The image of the human condition associated with the process model is one in which human beings have multiple possibilities for future action, yet face present conditions that tend to limit these possibilities. Thus, the central idea in the process model is that of human freedom.

The process model differs from the natural-law model because it does not picture a universe in which there are moral laws that exist regardless of human choice. It differs from the monist and pluralist models because it does not aim at the discovery of the factors that cause people to behave as they do. It holds that there are degrees of causation in human affairs and corresponding degrees of freedom. Natural law, monism, pluralism, and process represent distinctive ways of interpreting the human condition. In the following discussion each one of them will be considered from the viewpoint of one who seeks to clarify his vision of the human condition.

Natural Law

The central idea of natural law is that there is a moral order in the universe which binds human choice. Once a person has come to know this order through the use of reason, he also understands the pattern of human relations that is consistent with natural law. John Courtney Murray, a Catholic social thinker, has described the general features of natural law. First, natural law asserts that the nature of man is "a unitary and constant concept beneath all individual differences."[4] This means that, however much human beings appear to differ from one another, their ultimate fulfillment would be found in the realization of a purpose open to discovery by them. A consequence of this is that "for man, a rational being, the order of nature is not an order of necessity, to be fulfilled blindly, but an order of reason and therefore of freedom."[5]

Murray describes concretely what it means to take the natural-law viewpoint in everyday life. He considers the case of a man who is protesting against injustice where his own interests are not directly involved and where the injustice does not violate any civil law. An example would be someone protesting the denial of voting rights to eighteen-year-olds before the law was passed allowing them to vote. Murray argues that such a protestor is claiming that there is an idea of justice which exists apart from the will of any legislator and is rooted in the "nature of things." Further, Murray states that the protestor implies that he really knows this idea of justice, that it is not created by him but is instead an external standard for judging his action, that the idea should be realized in law and action, that its violation is unreasonable and "that this unreason is an offense not only against his own intelligence but against God, Who commands justice and forbids injustice."[6] Murray concludes that the protestor, who may know very little about social philosophy, "is thinking in the categories of natural law and in the sequence of ideas that the natural-law mentality (which is the human mentality) follows."[7]

Difficulties of The Natural-Law Viewpoint A first major difficulty with natural law is that it is possible to question whether or not the person engaged in political protest necessarily implies all the points listed by Murray. There is no doubt that the protestor makes his judgment that injustice has been done on the basis of a general standard of justice that he holds. This standard is often closely related to his vision of a good human condition. It is not clear, however, that the protestor necessarily claims that there is an idea of justice which exists apart from any particular human will and which is somehow rooted in the "nature of things." Instead, he may simply be claiming that he prefers to see a world in which the idea of justice that he holds is realized over a world in which this idea is not put into effect. This preference may be based on the judgment that he would feel better if his idea of justice was realized or that this idea of justice is part of a vision of the good life that he holds. If the protestor does not necessarily claim that his idea of justice is valid apart from any particular human will, he also does not imply that it is an external standard and that its violation is an offense against God. In fact, even if a person accepts natural law, he is not logically bound to accept the notion that God exists.

There is a second important difficulty in the natural-law position. While almost everybody may agree with such general maxims as "justice should be done," "equals should be treated equally," and "good should be sought and evil avoided," people may have serious disagreements about what is just, in what respects people should be deemed equal, and what is good. For example, some may hold that it is just to allow eighteen-year-olds to vote, while others may hold that such a privilege would create injustice. There seems to be nothing about the "nature of things" that would help in solving this dispute or in determining which camp was on the side of natural justice. This vagueness in natural law has made it a useful tool for groups seeking to defend or expand their rights and privileges. Defenders of the status quo have insisted that the current social order approximates the dictates of natural law, while those in favor of change have argued that the present order does not measure up to the standards of natural law. Sidney Hook has summed up this difficulty of the natural-law position: "Our own time has spawned a whole series of moral problems in which the right to security conflicts with the right to liberty and which challenges us to fruitful and creative devices that aim at giving us as much as possible of both but must on occasion risk our security or curb our freedom. The theory of natural law does not take us an inch forward in negotiating such conflicts."[8]

The natural-law position appears in a wide variety of forms in current social thought. Every person who claims that there are certain basic human needs which should be met, certain basic human rights which should be respected, or certain fixed standards of the social good or social justice which should guide action shares the natural-law position. Careful consideration of the preceding list will reveal that natural law remains the most widespread type of social thought in the contemporary world. Many people believe that there is a fixed "human nature" characterized by particular needs. Some people believe that these "needs" center around physical survival, and mainly include food, clothing, and shelter. Others hold that "man does not live by bread alone" and has "needs" for love or respect. Still others claim that human beings "need" to develop their potentialities to the fullest extent. Often the idea that human beings have certain inalienable rights goes along with the notion of human needs. Thus, some claim that there is a right to freedom from want, some assert a right to be treated with respect (or even to be loved), and some claim a right to full development. Frequently, such notions of needs and rights are turned into fixed standards of social good or social justice.

The Concept of Human Need It is worthwhile to spend some time on the idea of human need because it is at the root of most visions of the human condition. The central problem in notions of human need is that the supposed needs are not always met and there are people who seem not to want them to be met. For example, the most elementary need seems to be that for the means to continue physical existence. Most people agree that human beings "need" food, clothing, and shelter. However, while there is no dispute that these things are necessary for the continuation of physical existence, there is great disagreement about whether physical existence should be continued in all cases. There are people who say that they would rather be "dead than Red." Many others commit suicide for various reasons. Some governments spend more money on armaments than they do on encouraging the provision of food, clothing, and shelter. People go on hunger strikes to protest social conditions and even court death to further a cause. Others sacrifice their own lives in acts of heroism to save friends, relatives, or even total strangers. In each of these cases, of course, there is the assumption that some human beings will continue physical existence. However, there are people who believe that the universe would be better off without any human beings in it, and that the most noble human act would be to extinguish human life.

What does the person who holds the idea that human beings need food, clothing, and shelter say to the person who believes that human life should be destroyed? Frequently he says that this person is mentally ill, weird, perverted, deviant, abnormal, sinful, misguided, or some other term that makes the pessimist into less than a "real" human being. The assumption here is that anyone who does not fulfill the requirements set by a particular idea of human nature has thereby lost his standing as a human being. The usual follow-up to this judgment is either an attempt to make the deviant "see the light" or an effort to eradicate the deviant. These kinds of responses show how slippery the idea of human need can become. What begins as a call to universal good becomes an effort to liquidate the opposition, spiritually or physically.

Most natural-law thinkers draw consequences for social relations and group life from their descriptions of human nature. For example, Erich Fromm, who believes that the existence of human needs can be demonstrated scientifically, holds that women have a need to bear children: "Women have the power to bear children and to nurse them; if this power remains unused, if a woman does not become a mother, if she can not spend her power to bear and love a child, she experiences a frustration which can be remedied only by increased realization of her powers in other realms of her life."[9] How does one account for the childless woman who claims that she is not frustrated and who does not seem to be driven to achieve in other human activities?

A more serious application of natural law to social relations has been given by Mary Elizabeth Walsh and Paul Hanly Furfey. According to them, one learns how society ought to function by "examining its nature, that is, by studying what the thing essentially is."[10] They state that such an examination discloses that the common good implies the preservation of public order and the furtherance of economic and cultural welfare. Any deviation from these standards constitutes a social problem, and the denial of the natural law is itself "the root cause of modern social problems."[11] In the Catholic tradition of natural law that Walsh and Furfey represent, public order and economic and cultural welfare require monogamous marriage, the state, and the church. Where these institutions do not appear, human beings will not be able to attain the good life and will be living unnaturally and, therefore, unjustly. In the light of the earlier discussion it is appropriate to ask whether the necessity of particular institutions can be derived from such vague commandments as "preserve public order" and "further economic and cultural welfare."

The Western tradition of social thought has grown out of a natural-law basis. The Greek philosophers Plato and Aristotle both held conceptions of natural law that stressed that human reason could discover the principles of harmonious social relations. For Plato, justice meant each member of the community making the contribution for which he was best suited. Aristotle had a similar idea, but emphasized distribution of the social product to those who most deserved it and the participation of equals in making social decisions. In the Middle Ages natural law was tied to Christianity, and biblical revelation was viewed as a supplement to the principles of Plato and Aristotle. In modern times, natural law has become tied more and more to ideas of human need and mental health. Some thinkers like Branislaw Malinowski, Talcott Parsons, and Marion Levy have attempted to determine the "needs" that must be met if societies are to continue in existence. Others such as Erich Fromm, Sigmund Freud, Abraham Maslow, and Harry Stack Sullivan have attempted to determine the "needs" that must be met for the attainment of a "healthy personality." These examples show the persistence of natural law in contemporary social thought, although many of the thinkers would not so label their ideas.

Monism

Natural law thrives as an explicit social philosophy where people are relatively unaware of any other ways of life that might compete with their own. Where there is no immediate clash between alternative ways of organizing human relations and performing human activities, it is understandable that people might come to believe that their ways were just as natural as day succeeding night and apples falling from trees. Deviations from ordinary patterns of activity would be infrequent, and would likely be viewed as unnatural exceptions to the natural order. Such people would believe that their ways of organizing human life were part of the "nature of things."

When diverse peoples are thrown into contact with each other it becomes difficult to maintain a natural-law position unchallenged. Each of the different peoples is likely to hold that its way of life is part of the nature of things. In such a situation it becomes necessary to explain why those who follow different ways seem to violate "human nature" or the "natural law." Just such a situation happened at the end of the Middle Ages when, through the crusades and the age of exploration, Europeans were brought into extensive and intensive contact with the peoples of other continents. Over several centuries, two different approaches developed to account for the differences among ways of life. The first approach was monistic, in the sense that it explained the differences through a single factor or cause operating in variable conditions. The second approach was pluralistic, because it explained the differences through a multiplicity of conditions mutually determining a given result. Both monism and pluralism are responses of human beings in the modern age to the encounter of different ways of life and the growing complexity and specialization of human relations. The present section will treat monism and some of its particular varieties.

The hallmark of monism, and modern thought in general, is that it substitutes the problem of causation for the problem of the social ideal. According to natural law, "the social ideal springs from the very nature of human society itself."[12] When there is a clash of life-ways it becomes difficult to determine the "very nature" of human society. One can no longer look at his own community and see in it an image of the ideal. Confronted with this problem, some people do not abandon the search for the social ideal. They carry forward the natural-law tradition and frequently attempt to make it more universal. However, other people become concerned with a new problem: Why do people behave in such diverse ways? In his attempts to answer this question, the monist looks for an underlying cause or factor that will make sense out of all of the diversity.

Categories of Monism There are as many possible types of monism as there are different kinds of human activities, different human characteristics and different factors in the human environment. For example, some monists find economic, political, educational, or religious factors unifying the human condition. Others unify the human condition through such characteristics as race or sex. Still others believe that differences are accounted for by environmental "forces" such as geographical location or climate. In each case one part of human existence is separated out from all of the others and made the determinant of them.

Marxism The structure of monistic thought can best be illustrated by an example. Perhaps the most influential and compelling variety of monistic thought has been Marxism. Many social thinkers in the twentieth century owe an enormous debt to Marx for his detailed criticism of modern life. Numerous social thinkers since Marx can be usefully regarded as either revisionists of his thought or as critics reacting against it and substituting other interpretations. With the success of communist revolutions in many parts of the world, Marxism has become the official philosophy of regimes governing hundreds of millions of people. This fact alone makes Marxism the most significant variety of monism in the contemporary world.

The most accessible basic document of Marxism is the *Communist Manifesto,* drawn up as the platform of the Communist League, a workers' association, in 1848, shortly before the revolutions that took place in Europe during that year. The *Communist Manifesto* presents a monistic interpretation of the human condition based on the operation of economic factors in determining historical events.

The *Manifesto* begins with the assertion that the "history of all hitherto existing society is the history of class struggles."[13] For Karl Marx and Friedrich Engels, who wrote the *Manifesto,* class meant a group of people sharing a common relation to tools, or the means of producing goods and services. Whether or not one belongs to a certain class in the Marxist scheme of things depends upon one's relation to the ownership of the means of production and the types of tools that exist. In all historical societies there has been a continuous struggle between those who own and control the means of production and those who must depend on the owners for their survival. According to Marxists, the owners tend to exploit the rest of the population up to the point that such exploitation would threaten their very domination: "Hitherto, every form of society has been based . . . on the antagonism of oppressing and oppressed classes. But in order to oppress a class, certain conditions must be assured to it under which it can, at least, continue its slavish existence."[14] At bottom, exploitation means that the classes composed of owners attempt to appropriate for themselves all of what has been produced by the other classes beyond what is

A Brief Guide to Social Thought

necessary to continue the existence of these other classes as efficient producing units. Insofar as they are capable, the other classes attempt to fight against this exploitation.

Historical change comes about, in the Marxist model, through the rise of classes owning and controlling new and more efficient means of production. For example, the transition from the medieval to the modern era was accomplished by the bourgeoisie which controlled the means to international commerce and eventually the means to industrial manufacturing. The bourgeoisie, through a long series of struggles, was able to displace the hereditary land-owning nobility from its position as the dominant class. Ultimately, it gained its success because its members owned and controlled a form of productive property (the factory) which was a far more efficient means of production than the property (arable land) owned by the nobility.

Along with each dominant means of production goes an entire system of classes. In the Middle Ages, there was a multiplicity of classes. The nobility was the ruling class, gaining its importance from the ownership and control of land. Under the nobility were the vassals and serfs who, to a greater or lesser degree, were contractually bound to provide rents and services to their lord in return for the use of his land. In some cases, the serfs were attached to the land in the sense that they and their children were legally bound to work it unless released by their lord. Alongside the manor system were the towns, populated by merchants and skilled laborers who provided goods and services not available on the manor. It was from these merchants and laborers that the bourgeoisie grew.

After the triumph of the bourgeoisie through various legal and revolutionary conflicts, a new class system began to appear. According to Marx, this system would eventually develop to contain only two classes—the bourgeoisie and the proletariat. The bourgeoisie would centralize in their hands the ownership and control of all the means of production, and the proletariat, or working class, would have nothing to sell but their labor. Under these conditions, Marx thought, the bourgeoisie would no longer perform the function of organizing production and would become mere parasites on the rest of the population. Thus, there would be a sharp breach between those who owned the means of production and did no work and those who did all of the work, but did not own any tools. Under these conditions, Marx thought, there would be another series of revolutions in which the proletariat would displace the bourgeoisie and organize the means of production in its own interest. The interest of the proletariat, however, would be the interest of all, because there would no longer be any split between exploiters and workers. Humanity would be one, because people would no longer identify themselves first as members of a class and second as individuals.

The chief importance of Marxism as a monistic theory lies in the way that it organizes the whole of human activity around the idea of class, which in turn is based on economic differences. Such classes as the bourgeoisie and the proletariat are not simply groups based on ownership. They are also political groups, groups of thought, and groups with distinctive styles of life. This point is made strikingly in the *Manifesto* in a denunciation of the bourgeoisie: "Your very ideas are but the outgrowth of the conditions of your bourgeois production and bourgeois property, just as your jurisprudence is but the will of your class made into a law for all, a will whose essential character and direction are determined by the economic conditions of existence of your class."[15] Thus, for Marxists the diversity of human existence becomes understandable when it is organized by economic factors.

Monism's Attractions Like natural law, monistic social thought has many attractions. First, well-thought-out doctrines like Marxism are able to make a great deal of sense out of apparently disconnected events by fitting them into a single pattern. Monistic thinkers often provide new and fresh perspectives on everyday life. For example, many people in sympathy with the women's liberation movement have been impressed by Marx' observation: "The bourgeois sees in his wife a mere instrument of production."[16] These insights, though often partial, are helpful in fashioning a coherent vision of the human condition. Second, monistic thinkers provide a direction for human action. If economic relations pattern all of the other human relations, then social changes will come through the alteration of economic relations. This kind of reasoning has given social movements based on monistic doctrines a clarity of program lacking in other movements. Third, monistic theories are attractive because of their seeming realism. Marx called himself a "scientific" socialist who had discovered the causes of historical change rather than a "utopian" socialist who would dream about ideal communities, but never think seriously about what would be necessary to put them into effect.

Monism's Difficulties There are two major problems in monistic theories. The first stems from the effort to organize all of human existence around a single activity. Even with respect to such a compelling view as Marxism, does it make sense to claim that such a factor as economic conditions underlies the whole of human affairs? For example, take the observation that the bourgeois sees in his wife a mere instrument of production. While there may be some people in the ownership classes who view their wives merely as machines for producing children, objects for giving them physical pleasure, and trophies of their success in the rat race, these kinds of relations do not exhaust the possibilities within marriage in the industrial age. There are many other attitudes and viewpoints embodied in bourgeois marriages, such as cooperative sharing of experience, mutual support, and development of common interests. This does not mean that the typical modern view of the woman is as a full person. With great frequency women are treated as mere instruments of production and consumption, and this conception is enshrined in religion, literature, and political thought.[17] However, it is inaccurate to reduce the condition of women to economic relations, and this inaccuracy frequently results in actual blocks to the realization of personal freedom.

Suppose that someone points out that he does not treat his wife as a mere instrument of production, and that his wife agrees with this judgment. Suppose, further, that an impartial outside observer also agrees with the judgment. Confronted with this evidence, a dogmatic Marxist might try to search for any evidence of exploitation in the relationship. If he found evidence of exploitation he might say that this meant that the entire relationship was oppressive. If he found no evidence of oppression he might still say that exploitation was "really" there whether or not it was obvious or even discoverable after long investigation. This conclusion would mean that nothing could convince the dogmatic Marxist that a bourgeois marriage could be founded on anything but exploitation. Such a conclusion, if accepted by the people involved, would block their realization of personal freedom because it would destroy their confidence in their own powers of critical judgment. Thus, through attempting to account for all human activity through the operation of a single factor, extreme monism leads to factual inaccuracy and blocks to freedom.

The second difficulty with monism is related to the first. It concerns the notion that a person's very ideas are the outgrowth of the so-called driving factor in human existence. While there are profound connections between work and thought, and while becoming aware of these connections increases the range of freedom, thought cannot necessarily be reduced to some non-conscious factor. Stating that thought is caused by economic relations frequently leads to the denial of reasoned conversation. For example, two people may claim that their marriage is based on the development of common interests. A dogmatic Marxist may respond, "You are only saying that because you are members of the bourgeoisie, and your class position determines your ideas." This kind of response is equivalent to the idea that a person is mentally ill or evil if he does not hold someone's idea of natural law. It makes people lose respect for their minds.

Monism is very important in contemporary life. It takes many other forms than economic determinism, but is always characterized by the belief that a single factor unites the diverse aspects of the human condition. The coherence gained by concentrating on a single theme, however, frequently involves the sacrifice of factual accuracy and the expansion of freedom.

Pluralism

Pluralism arose as a response to some of the problems in monistic thought described in the preceding section. Some social thinkers were struck by the fact that the single-factor interpretations of monism often stretched the imagination by distorting events to fit the preconceived mold. Others were disturbed by the tendency of monists to claim that their pet factors were responsible for causing events when no such connection appeared to be discoverable. Still others were concerned with the ways in which monistic theories seemed to limit freedom by claims that certain future events, such as the displacement of the bourgeoisie by the proletariat, were inevitable regardless of human choice. All monistic theories seemed to lead to a paradox. The social movements based on them made frantic efforts to recruit followers while at the same time proclaiming the inevitability of their success. Explanations that such recruiting was done to make the inevitable happen sooner were not entirely satisfactory. Together, these criticisms formed the basis of pluralist thought.

The most basic assumption of pluralism is that a large number of factors determines human events, rather than a single dominant theme. However, if this claim was all there was to pluralism it could not be considered a serious type of social thought. There is a kind of crude pluralism that appears in everyday life and in political propaganda that criticizes Marxism and other monistic theories by stating simply that "reality is far more complex than the Marxists would have it." From these kinds of remarks one is supposed to draw the conclusion that all efforts at major social change are misguided. Crude pluralists tend to believe that out of the competition between social groups grows a balance of interests and a progressive solution to social problems. Crude pluralism is the doctrine contained in most American propaganda and, therefore, should not be confused with pluralism as a major type of social thought. It sidesteps any serious encounter with monistic theories through a vague idea of "complexity," while serious pluralism reworks the root assumptions of monism.

Once certain social thinkers adopted the idea of multifactor causation of human events, they were faced with the serious problem of how to compare these factors to one another. There was wide agreement that economic factors, as well as political, religious, familial, educational, and other factors played a part in determining the character of the human condition. However, comparing these factors to one another seemed like comparing apples and oranges. In order to make any sense out of the multitude of factors (something that crude pluralists do not care to do) the serious pluralists set out to discover a basis for comparison, or what the various factors had in common.

The results of this search were a series of concepts that have become the basis of contemporary sociology. What the search revealed appears to be quite simple, but was in fact revolutionary in the changes it accomplished in social thought. The pluralists discovered that all of the major factors suggested in the monistic theories were forms of human activity. The economic factor was the activity of producing and distributing goods and services. The political factor was the activity of making decisions and trying to see that they were carried out. The educational factor was the activity of transmitting information from one person to another. These factors and many others were responsible for the pattern of human events, but they were all activities.[18]

The discovery that human activity underlies all the particular factors suggested by monistic theories was an impressive advance in thought because it removed social thought from what is immediately visible in the commonsense world. A moment's thought will show that one never encounters human activity in general in everyday life. One always encounters a particular type of human activity, whether it be economic, political, religious, educational, or some other. Thus, for pluralists activity itself is the *form* of social life, while each particular activity is distinguished by a particular *content* (production, communication, or some other). The distinctions between form and content are not, of course, absolute. For example, the particular activity of production is never encountered in everyday life. One always finds people producing something specific. Thus, the activity of production is in this case the *form* of economic activity, while the *content* of economic activity varies according to what is being produced (automobiles, color-television sets, machine guns, or some other objects).

The reasoning behind pluralist thought discloses its major departure from monist thought. Monistic perspectives attempt to unify the diverse aspects of the human condition around a single factor or content. Pluralistic perspectives attempt to unify the various aspects of the human condition around the forms common to all contents. This difference can be illustrated by considering briefly how Marxism is revised by pluralist thought.

The Pluralist's View of Marxism The central idea of Marxism is that the history of all hitherto existing society is the history of class struggles. The pluralist thinker would change this sentence to read, "The history of all hitherto existing society is the history of group relations." According to the pluralist all human activity takes place within the context of groups. Among these groups are classes, as defined by Marx. However, the classes may not be the most important groups in every situation. Sometimes family groups, religious sects, or schools of thought are more important than economic classes in determining the character of human existence. Further, the pluralist would argue that struggle is only one form of human relationship. In addition to struggle and conflict, there are also such relationships as cooperation, competition, exchange, and love. There is no guarantee that struggle will be the most important human relation in all cases. The pluralist holds that the only way of finding out which group or which relation is the most important in a particular situation is to go out and investigate that situation. Thus, pluralistic thought attempts to make no assumptions about the dominant factors in the human condition in advance of investigation.

Most of the discussion that follows will be based on the contributions of pluralistic thinkers, because they have dominated twentieth-century sociology. Sociologists such as Max Weber, Emile Durkheim, George Herbert Mead, Vilfredo Pareto, Gaetano Mosca, Georg Simmel, Arthur F. Bentley, and Talcott Parsons identified different aspects of human activity that overarch the particular factors contained in monistic social thought. Their works contain images of the contemporary human condition that put into order many of the problems that people confront today. These images will not be considered at this point because they will be revealed throughout the following discussion.

Pluralism's Problems Like the other types of social thought, pluralism has difficulties. They center around the idea that the task of social thought is to find the conditions that determine human events. Some pluralists tend to believe that it is possible to look at the human condition from the outside, like a geologist inspects a rock, and find out what factors gave it the character it displays. Thus, they often forget that they themselves are actors in the human condition, and that their very social thought is a guide to social action. Like every other type of social thought, pluralism is both a description of the human condition and a way of orienting activity within that condition. In natural law and monism, it is clear how social thought performs this double function. Natural-law thinkers claim to describe a series of human needs and a set of social relations for meeting these needs. Thus, natural law serves as a guide to action by orienting people to creating or perfecting the relations required for satisfying human needs. Similarly, monistic thinkers claim to describe a single force around which all social relations can be organized. Thus, monistic thought serves as a guide to action by showing people what factors they should take account of in their efforts to gain certain social changes. For example, as a guide to action, Marxism directs one to work upon economic conditions, rather than the religious life or some other factor, to effect desired changes.

It is more difficult to show how pluralism is a guide to action, because most pluralists believe that they are simply describing and explaining human events, rather than orienting action toward those events. However, pluralist thinking does give rise to a distinctive type of action. According to the pluralist, there can be no conclusive judgments made in advance of observation and experimentation about the factor that is most important in determining a given human situation. This means that the adoption of pluralism prevents one from subscribing to any particular variety of monistic thought. Further, the pluralist finds human activity to be the basic factor unifying the human condition, and cannot adopt any particular natural-law interpretation of social relations. For him, there is no hidden set of needs lurking behind activity and experience.

How, then, does pluralism serve as a guide to action? Since pluralists can neither assume that any particular factor is of decisive importance in determining the human condition nor claim that a fixed set of needs characterizes human nature, they must adopt an experimental attitude toward human existence. They must treat every natural law and monistic perspective as a possible social experiment. For example, Marxism could be treated as an experiment in transforming social relations through collective action on economic conditions. The human condition itself would be the laboratory for social experimentation. Further, pluralists must treat their own pluralism as an experiment in taking an experimental attitude. Thus, pluralism demands that all types of social thought be viewed as possible guides to action. This recognition that each vision of the human condition is a guide to action as well as a description demands an assumption that human beings are free to choose among competing visions. Through their choices, human beings help determine which interpretation of the human condition will come true. It is this fact that makes it difficult for pluralists to claim that they are merely outside observers seeking the causes of human events. The idea that pluralism is a guide to action, counseling experimentalism rather than dogmatism, and that it is one guide to action among many, leads directly to the process pattern of social thought.

PROCESS

Process thought arises in response to conditions in the contemporary world that are equal in their impact to the encounter of diverse ways of life that led to the development of monistic and pluralistic perspectives. Talcott Parsons has noted that the primary question that modern (monistic and pluralistic) thinkers sought to answer was the problem of order: How is society possible?[19] Impressed by the conflicts brought about by European exploration and exploitation of the rest of the world, and by progressive specialization and industrialization, modern thinkers were concerned to discover how human beings avoided a chaotic war of all against all. Three general answers were developed to this question. One group of thinkers held that the stability of human relations was secured by superior might and wealth. Marx was one representative of this position. A second group held that the order present in human relations was sustained by agreement on the rules of social living. Many pluralists have held this position. In its most popular form it asserts that, through rewards for conforming to the rules and punishments for breaking them, human beings learn to obey the standards prevailing in social groups. In this process of learning, so its advocates argue, people come to believe that the prevailing standards are right and that they have an obligation to obey them. The ideas that stability results from exploitation and that order is maintained by agreement on rules of conduct are not in necessary conflict with each other, unless either one is defined as the only answer to the problem of order. Thus, a third group of social thinkers, the most numerous, has argued that both might and agreement are factors in the maintenance of social order.

In the twentieth century, there has been an increasing challenge to the idea that the central question in social thought is the problem of order. Part of the reason for this challenge is contained in the fact that in recent decades for many people order has not appeared to be the greatest problem in social life. The twentieth century has witnessed the growth of enormous organizations, or conglomerates, performing a multitude of functions, in which decisions affecting the lives of millions of people are made on a daily basis. For some of those who are workers within the conglomerates such as the state, the large university, or the multinational corporation, and for those who feel the consequences of their decisions, there is no problem of order—the lives of these people are structured by an order that is beyond their ability to control. Further, as time goes on more reports appear of drugs that can be used to control moods and behaviors, of improved propaganda and brainwashing methods, and of the accumulation by conglomerates of information on peoples' lives. In the face of these conditions it is understandable that a number of people have no difficulty in believing how order is possible.

The new question that has arisen to challenge the problem of order can be called the problem of liberation. Rather than asking how society is possible in a world of diversity and conflicting individual and group interests, the process thinkers are concerned with how freedom is possible in a world increasingly dominated by mammoth organizations. The emergence of patterns of social thought based on answers to the problem of freedom shows how closely social thought is tied to events and characteristics in other sectors of the human condition. Throughout the world, people have become aware of the problem of liberation. People throughout Asia, Africa, and Latin America are demanding liberation from order imposed by the nations of Europe and Anglo-America. Minority, sex, and age groups within Europe and Anglo-America are demanding liberation from order imposed by dominant groups on these continents. Rebels within the Soviet bloc are demanding liberation from controls on freedom of expression and freedom of political participation. Individuals throughout the world are demanding liberation from the constraints on their thought and action imposed by the conglomerates. This worldwide movement for liberation has impressed many twentieth-century social thinkers in much the same way that the encounter with diversity and complexity impressed social thinkers of past centuries.

Process thought is based upon the central premise that the human condition is unified by a single process of action. This process of action is defined by the fact that human beings can reject their present conditions in favor of a vision of the future. Herbert Marcuse has called this fact "the power of negative thinking" because it discloses the ability of human beings to deny that their present conditions are necessary and must inevitably continue.[20] Bound up with this notion is the idea that the human process has four dimensions.

Four Dimensions Inherent in the Human Process The first dimension is *lived experience*. Lived experience means that human beings are directly aware of their feelings and of the constant transformation they undergo. Human beings are aware of time through felt organic change. Their original experience is of feelings. The second dimension is *social experience*. This means that the human process involves social relations such as competition, cooperation, conflict, and love. Through such relations people become aware that they are different from their environment and from other human beings. The third dimension is *cultural experience*. This is the aspect of meaning in the human process. Out of experience, human beings create and carve objects they can use over and over again to produce similar results. The set of these objects is culture, and the complexes of culture provide people with opportunities to store and stabilize experience. Finally, the fourth dimension is *creative experience*. While cultural experience is the appreciation of objects created in the past, creative experience is the generation and use of new meaningful objects.

In sum, the human process involves people experiencing in common, acting in relation to one another, using meaningful objects and continually creating anew the conditions for their existence. It is this idea of the human process that underlies the present book.

The preceding description of the human process reveals a great deal about the interpretation of the problem of freedom in the twentieth century. For the existentialists, the pragmatists, and the humanists who disclosed the various dimensions of this process, freedom is something positive.[21] In one way or another each thinker who has attempted to respond to the problem of freedom has challenged the idea of vacant freedom which has been so popular in the modern era.[22] Vacant freedom is the notion that freedom is merely the absence of all restraints. It is the cry of all those who seek freedom *from* domination. However, vacant freedom by itself contains little satisfaction for human beings. It is the freedom that appears when a person has nothing left to do. If they clarify their images of the human condition, most people discover that behind their struggle to gain freedom from domination is a quest after freedom *for* something. The process thinkers have attempted to describe the aspects of "freedom for" and to show the possibilities for such freedom in the present human condition.

Some Details of Human Freedom One aspect of "freedom for" is *clarification* of one's vision of the human condition. Without such clarification one's consciousness remains merely a bundle of desires and myths without any rhyme or reason. A second aspect of positive freedom is *generalization of the vision,* which allows one to identify the group that is composed of one's allies. The third aspect of freedom for is *relativization,* which allows one to identify competing groups and visions. Finally, the fourth aspect of positive freedom is *commitment,* or the decision to act upon an image of a future human condition after the consideration of one's own ideas and the ideas of others. For the thinkers who have attempted to deal seriously with the problem of freedom, any worthwhile vision of the human condition will include the project to continue, deepen and extend the process of self-examination. They find it is this very process that is discouraged by the massive conglomerates of the contemporary world, whose propaganda systematically distorts the human condition and aims at lulling human beings into complacency and obedience. In the nineteenth century Marx could declare: "Workers of the world unite, you have nothing to lose but your chains." Today in the face of propaganda, advertising, and other forms of mental manipulation the process thinkers tell us: "Examine yourselves and your society, you have your minds to gain." Thus, in the end, *freedom for* means well founded respect for one's mind.

Process thought does not reject the contributions of natural law, monism and pluralism, but reinterprets them. It makes the needs of the natural-law thinker into possibilities for human action. It makes the causes of the monists and the pluralists into aspects of the human condition that must be taken account of in any attempts at intelligent action. It also asserts that human beings have some control over whether or not they will make such factors as economic conditions central in their lives. In sum, it finds in the fact that all types of social thought are both guides for action and descriptions of action evidence for the existence of a process of self-examination; it is this that opens the door to positive freedom.

Figure 2.1. THE TYPES OF SOCIAL THOUGHT

Natural Law:	Defines a set of human needs and devises a social ideal in which these needs would be met
Monism:	Defines a single factor in human existence which supposedly accounts for social relations and organization
Pluralism:	Explains social relations and organization through a multiplicity of factors
Process:	Organizes social relations and organization around a single human process of freedom

SOCIAL THOUGHT IN REVIEW

There are many possible maps of social thought. The one presented above is especially adapted to aiding the process of self-examination. It identifies four general types of social thought, each based on a different image of the human condition. While there may be other types of social thought than the ones identified and, therefore, other visions of the human condition, these four have appeared most frequently in the history of civilizations, both East and West. In order to simplify the process of self-examination, one should attempt to discover whether his own thought fits roughly into any one of these four patterns and then read more deeply the works of a writer who develops that pattern. Although the idea of process guides this book, there is no reason why one has to adopt this pattern. We would be acting in bad faith if we did not attempt to defend the type of thought which we think is most sound. However, many intelligent and thoughtful people disagree with us on fundamental issues, and it is worth your while to find out what serious natural-law thinkers, monists, and pluralists have to say. You may very well adhere to one of these three patterns, particularly natural law or monism, and you may end up sticking to your position. It is up to you to find out.

To sum up, natural-law thinkers attempt to answer the question, "What is the good life?" Their answer is usually that the good life is the fulfillment of some basic human "needs" that they have identified. In one form or another, natural law was the dominant form of social thought up until modern times. It is still probably the most widespread perspective, since most people believe that there is some such thing as "mental health" or "moral goodness," that can be defined with precision. Pluralism and monism arose in the modern era, primarily as a response to the breakdown of the older traditions and the growing diversity in the human condition. Monistic theorists searched for a single cause or factor that would account for the observed differences in human life and would explain why stability in human relations was maintained in the face of fierce conflicts. Pluralistic theorists claimed that a multitude of factors determined the precise character of the human condition, and unified thought about human relations around the idea of human activity. Growing out of monism and pluralism, process thought has analyzed the idea of human activity and has found that it is based on a notion of human process which involves positive freedom. The possibilities for such freedom have become particularly important for many people in the twentieth century who are less interested in how order can be maintained than they are concerned with how to win liberation from powerful organizations.

As one studies social thought with a view to its effects on one's own thought and action, it is important to know the standards by which it can be evaluated. The discussion of such standards is the aim of the next chapter.

A Sampler of Theorists

The following list of theorists is a small sampling of representatives of the four perspectives discussed in this chapter: natural law, monism, pluralism, and process. It may be used as a beginning in the attempt to clarify one's own vision of social structure and human relations. Select the perspective which seems closest to your own, choose a theorist from the list, and as you read the work identify the points at which you agree and disagree with the presentation. If you follow this process through you should be able to clarify your own assumptions about society and then be ready to appreciate other perspectives.

Natural Law Scientific sociology was, in part, a rebellion against natural-law theories of society. There are therefore, few representatives of this perspective in contemporary sociology. Older religious visions of natural law still survive, however, and to them have been added theories of the "normal" or healthy self derived from personality theory.

RELIGIOUS INTERPRETATIONS

FURFEY, PAUL HANLY. *Three Theories of Society*. New York: Macmillan, 1937. Furfey criticizes the model of society promoted by scientific sociology and attempts to show how sociological theories imply moralities. He then introduces a traditional interpretation of natural law as an alternative sociological theory and morality.

MARITAIN, JACQUES. *Scholasticism and Politics*. Garden City, N.Y.: Image Books, 1960. Maritain attempts to apply traditional natural law to contemporary social problems, tracing these problems to an erosion of public morality.

PSYCHOLOGICAL INTERPRETATIONS

FREUD, SIGMUND. *Civilization and Its Discontents*. New York: W. W. Norton, 1961. Freud traces contemporary social conflicts to repressed instincts and drives.

FROMM, ERICH. *The Revolution of Hope: Toward a Humanized Technology.* New York: Harper & Row, 1968. Fromm presents a critique of contemporary institutions based on a view of the healthy personality.

Monism   Monism was the characteristic perspective of nineteenth-century sociology. While pluralistic and process theories have displaced it in the mainstream of contemporary American sociology, there are still many monists, particularly Marxists, who are actively theorizing. Monisms may be divided according to the key factors which they stress in their interpretations of social life.

ECONOMIC MONISMS

MARCUSE, HERBERT. *Negations.* Boston: Beacon Press, 1968. Marcuse adapts a basically Marxist view to contemporary organizational society.

MARX, KARL, and ENGELS, FRIEDRICH. *The Communist Manifesto.* New York: Appleton-Century-Crofts, 1955. This is still the most accessible and best introduction to economic monism.

TECHNOLOGICAL MONISMS

CHILDE, V. GORDON. *Man Makes Himself.* New York: New American Library, 1951. Childe presents an interpretation of civilization based on successive technological innovations.

VEBLEN, THORSTEIN. *The Theory of the Leisure Class.* New York: New American Library, 1953. Veblen's classic is a critique of the predatory nature of modern society.

GEOPHYSICAL MONISMS

HUNTINGTON, ELLSWORTH. *Mainsprings of Civilization.* New York: New American Library, 1959. Huntington analyzes the role of biological inheritance and physical environment in influencing the course of history.

WITTFOGEL, KARL A. *Oriental Despotism.* New Haven: Yale University Press, 1957. Wittfogel links the appearance of absolutist bureaucratic regimes to the need to coordinate agricultural production.

BIORACIAL MONISMS

CHAMBERLAIN, HOUSTON STEWART. *Foundations of the Nineteenth Century.* New York: Dodd, Mead, 1912. Chamberlain's defense of the Germanic or Aryan "race" was a source of much Nazi propaganda.

STORR, ANTHONY. *Human Aggression.* New York: Atheneum, 1968. Storr draws conclusions from ethology (the study of animal behavior) about the nature of human social organization.

POSITIVISTIC MONISMS

DEGRANGE, MACQUILKIN. *The Nature and Elements of Sociology.* New Haven: Yale University Press, 1953. DeGrange attempts to bring Auguste Comte's positivism and his theory of the stages of human society and understanding up to date.

WHITE, LESLIE A. *The Science of Culture.* New York: Farrar, Straus & Young, 1949. White presents a positivistic theory of historical evolution heavily laced with technological monism.

Pluralism Pluralism is the dominant perspective in twentieth-century sociology. Like natural law and monism, it is not a homogeneous perspective, but is characterized by a number of different emphases. Some pluralists are interested primarily in the conflict among diverse groups, others are concerned with the ways in which some groups dominate others, others are concerned with how different social activities are integrated together, others are interested in patterns of organizational coordination, and others are concerned with the formation of the human self out of social relations.

CONFLICT APPROACH

DAHRENDORF, RALF. *Class and Class Conflict in Industrial Society.* Stanford: Stanford University Press, 1959. Dahrendorf "pluralizes" Marx by pointing to a number of conflicts in contemporary society.

SIMMEL, GEORG. *Conflict and the Web of Group Affiliation.* New York: Free Press, 1955. Simmel describes the various forms which conflict takes in social life.

ELITE AND DOMINATION APPROACH

MANNHEIM, KARL. *Man and Society in an Age of Reconstruction.* New York: Harcourt, Brace, 1940. Mannheim presents an argument for elite planning in a multi-group society.

PARETO, VILFREDO. *Sociological Writings.* New York: Frederick A. Praeger, 1966. Pareto "pluralizes" Marx by analyzing elitism and domination as general social phenomena.

FUNCTIONALIST OR INTEGRATIVE APPROACH

DURKHEIM, EMILE. *The Division of Labor in Society.* New York: Free Press, 1947. Durkheim "pluralizes" Marx by outlining the general forms of "solidarity," or the way diverse activities in society are coordinated.

PARSONS, TALCOTT. *The Social System.* New York: Free Press, 1951. Parsons presents a general theory of social control, emphasizing the way social roles are integrated into systems of coordinated action through the coordination of sanctions.

ORGANIZATIONAL APPROACH

GERTH, H. H., and MILLS, C. WRIGHT. *From Max Weber.* New York: Oxford University Press, 1958. Weber "pluralizes" Marx by outlining a general pattern of hierarchical organization characteristic of modern societies—the bureaucracy.

BLAU, PETER M., and SCOTT, W. RICHARD. *Formal Organizations.* San Francisco: Chandler, 1962. Blau and Scott "pluralize" Weber by pointing out structural dilemmas within organizations as well as the dynamics of "informal organizations" which grow up around formal structures.

SOCIAL PSYCHOLOGICAL APPROACH

MEAD, GEORGE H. *Mind, Self, and Society.* Chicago: University of Chicago Press, 1934. Mead describes how the self is formed through interaction with other human beings and how people are "socialized" to obey the rules of the "game."

GOFFMAN, ERVING. *The Presentation of Self in Everyday Life.* Garden City: N.Y.: Doubleday, 1959. Goffman shows how people engage in "impression management" to regulate their relations with others.

Process Process theory, the most recent general perspective in sociological analysis, has, like the other frameworks, several distinct foci of concern. Some thinkers are primarily concerned with the types of human activity, others are interested in analyzing the images and perspectives through which people view their social life, others are concerned with the principles of contemporary social structure and others are interested in the possible patterns of relations ("dialectics") which can characterize intergroup and interpersonal activity.

ACTIVITY FOCUS

BENTLEY, ARTHUR F. *Relativity in Man and Society.* New York: G. P. Putnam's Sons, 1926. Bentley describes human society as an interlacing of cross sections of activity and presents a method of "socioanalysis" similar to the process of self-understanding described in this book.

ZNANIECKI, FLORIAN. *The Cultural Sciences.* Urbana: University of Illinois Press, 1952. Building the idea of creative activity into his analysis, Znaniecki presents a general theory of culture and society.

EPISTEMOLOGICAL (PERSPECTIVAL) FOCUS

NORTHROP, F. S. C. *The Meeting of East and West.* New York: Collier Books, 1966. Northrop shows how different cultures express different theories of knowledge and experience.

SOROKIN, PITIRIM. *Sociological Theories of Today.* New York: Harper & Row, 1966. Sorokin presents a review of contemporary sociological theories from a perspective similar to Northrop's.

SOCIAL-ORGANIZATION FOCUS

JORDAN, ELIJAH. *Business Be Damned.* New York: Henry Schuman, 1952. Jordan offers a scathing critique of contemporary social institutions from the viewpoint of a philosophy of creative freedom.

HILLER, E. T. *The Nature and Basis of Social Order.* New Haven: College and University Press, 1966. Following from Jordan's critique of the privatization of contemporary society, Hiller applies the notion of human process to a theory of social organization.

DIALECTICAL FOCUS

GURVITCH, GEORGES. *Dialectique et Sociologie.* Paris: Flammarion, 1962. Gurvitch shows how dialectical analysis of social relations is consistent with a process of creative freedom. See also, Philip Bosserman's commentary on Gurvitch's sociology, published in English.

MUKERJEE, RADHAKAMAL. *The Philosophy of Social Science.* London: Macmillan, 1960. Like Gurvitch, Mukerjee develops a multifaceted dialectic and coordinates it with a theory of social structure and a philosophy of freedom.

3
SOCIOLOGY AND SCIENCE

The first two chapters of this book contain an introduction to thinking about the human condition. The first chapter shows that to understand oneself fully it is necessary to understand the social situation in which one is acting. The way to attain such understanding is to clarify one's vision of the human condition, generalize it and relativize it with respect to the images held by others, and then commit oneself to the resulting vision and start the process all over again. The second chapter describes various images of the human condition that have been held in the past and that have adherents at the present time, with the aim of making the process of self-understanding more easy to undertake.

Throughout these first two chapters an important question has been left unanswered, even unasked: Are there any standards for choosing among competing visions of the human condition? We believe that the answer is yes. If we thought that the answer was no, or even maybe, we would probably not have written this book, because we would have despaired that the process of self-examination led nowhere but to a bottomless pit. Our affirmative answer to the question is based on a judgment that the investigation of human affairs can be scientific. Thus, the standards for choosing among competing visions of the human condition are rooted in science, and to grasp those standards it is necessary to understand what is meant by a human science.[1]

SCIENCE

Science (and, somehow, particularly, the term social science) is terminology that frightens and mystifies many people. It is, of course, one of the major aims of this chapter to dispel this fear and worship because we would like everyone to become a sociologist, at least in the sense that we would like everyone continually to reexamine the human condition in a critical way. This means that we believe that everyone who is reading this book is capable of understanding the scientific method and applying it to his own existence.

The fear and awe that the term science awakens is due to a narrow and distorted interpretation of scientific activity. According to this distorted interpretation, scientists carve up human experience into distinct and highly specialized fields, invent terms to describe events that only they can understand, and then provide information to engineers who invent machines that nobody can control.[2] It is no wonder that those who have such a view of science stand in awe of it. Yet this interpretation of science only describes a very small part of scientific inquiry. At the heart of science is a series of standards for evaluating thought, and these standards have little to do with specialized fields, mysterious languages, and complicated machines. The scientific method and scientific standards are available to all for use in their daily lives, not just to a new caste of academic priests. This should be kept in mind whenever anyone tries to browbeat you into doing something that you do not understand on the grounds that it is in some way "scientific."

The best way of understanding the scientific method as it applies to the study of human affairs is to view it as an answer to the question, By what standards does one evaluate an image of the human condition? There are four general standards for evaluating a vision of the human condition—accuracy, consistency, adequacy, and fruitfulness. These standards will each be discussed in turn.

ACCURACY

Probably the first response that most people would give to the question of evaluating images of the human condition is that they would apply a standard of truth. Usually what is meant by "truth" is factual accuracy. Do the word pictures that make up the vision describe what is really going on? For example, is Marx correct that there is a connection between class position and what people think about human relations? This kind of question, which at first appears easy to answer, hides a great many difficulties. Awareness of these difficulties allows a person to apply better the standard of factual accuracy to his image of the human condition.

Many people in the United States have a love affair with facts. This attitude is strikingly illustrated by Sergeant Friday, hero of the old television police drama, "Dragnet." Friday would spend his time tracking down criminals by interviewing witnesses and other leads. Whenever the individual who he was questioning would wander off the subject and start talking about personal opinions, feelings or theories, Friday would sharply say, "Just the facts!" There are many Sergeant Fridays in the United States, in all walks of life. They believe that the world rests on a solid bedrock of fact and become very impatient when they believe that their associates are ignoring this bedrock in favor of cloudlike "pleasing illusions." Yet Sergeant Friday should have known that the "facts" cannot be easily separated from opinions, feelings, or theories.

A good police detective knows that the facts are rarely obvious. Suppose a murder has been committed in front of a crowd of people. Perhaps the most that everyone in the crowd will agree with is that someone is dead. When the police are summoned, some people in the crowd will tell them that the killing was surely done in self-defense. Others will say that it was certainly the case that cold-blooded murder was committed. Some will say that the killer was tall and thin, while others will state that he was short and fat. Others will not be sure whether it was a man or a woman who did the killing. "Positive identification" of the killer will prove to be very difficult, as will even the description of the killing itself. As time goes on, memories of the event will become vague in the minds of onlookers or, worse, some of them will begin to believe that they are certain about things that at the time of the killing they were in doubt about. When it comes time to question "leads," so-called facts will often count for far less than "theories." There will be an attempt to determine motivation for the killing. Thus, part of the investigation will focus on the opinions that people have about the suspects, their ideas about possible motivations and even their feelings. (The amazingly different interpretations and recollections on the Watergate-related events are another vivid example of this phenomenon.)

The situation becomes far more complex when a suspect is arrested and tried for the crime. The defense may attempt to argue that there was not any crime committed, and that the killing was in self-defense. Or, it may argue that while the defendant did the killing he was insane at the time. Of course, it may argue that the defendant is not the killer, and try to "prove" its case by questioning the testimony of prosecution witnesses, bringing in witnesses of its own, questioning the motives brought up by the prosecution and calling upon "expert" witnesses to demonstrate that it was "impossible" for the defendant to have committed the murder. The prosecution will call upon its own set of "facts" which will often be completely at odds with those brought up by the defense. Some of the so-called facts relied upon by each side will be considered "evidence" and, thus, will be allowed to count towards a verdict. Others will not be allowed into evidence and will not be allowed to count towards a verdict, because they will not measure up to a legally valid fact. It is the presence of rules of evidence that points up more than anything else in the administration of law the difficulty of determining the "facts" in complex human situations.[3]

Another indication that fact is not always obvious is the care with which juries are often selected. Each side tries to get people on the jury who are predisposed toward its case. They do this not because they believe that human beings are cynical creatures who invariably let the interest in truth be obscured by passion, but because they know that prejudices and predispositions color one's interpretations of the "facts" and lead to selectivity in which facts will be deemed important. When a verdict is reached in a complex case, then, it is not at all certain that the relevant facts were brought out, or considered in reaching the verdict.

Why spend so much time on an example from legal administration when the aim is describing the role of fact in science? The answer is that fact is no more obvious in science than it is in law. Before it is possible to get the facts, it is necessary to know what one is looking for. This means that the facts normally *succeed* rather than *precede* images of the human condition.[4] Since this idea runs against what most people consider "common sense" it is necessary to inspect it more closely.

Problems in Acquiring Facts When Sergeant Friday asked for "just the facts" he got both more and less than he bargained for. He got more than he bargained for because the people who responded to his questions gave him their interpretations of the event along with the "facts" about it. He got less than he bargained for because he conducted the investigation with a certain view of what was relevant. Thus, his questions were determined by a notion of what it is important to find out when one is conducting a criminal investigation. This means that he was likely to miss out on some facts that did not fit into the framework of his questions. The scientist studying human affairs is in no different position from Sergeant Friday. If he is in search of the "pure facts" he also gets more and less than he bargains for.[5] He gets more than he bargains for because, like Sergeant Friday, he is normally considering the interpretations that people give to events as well as the events themselves. This makes him differ somewhat from the natural scientist who, if he is studying squirrels, does not have to take account of the squirrel's beliefs about his own behavior. He gets less than he bargains for because he is always approaching his study with a certain framework of questions in mind. It is this aspect of a framework that is most important in the judgment that facts succeed rather than precede images of the human condition.[6]

In the second chapter we showed that in the twentieth century some social thinkers have shifted from concern with the problem of order to an interest in the problem of freedom. This shift will illustrate how facts tend to follow frameworks or images. Those social thinkers who are most concerned with the problem of order tend to look for facts that will support proposed solutions to this problem. For example, those who believe that order is maintained through exploitation will look for the instances in which human beings are controlled by such means as force, fraud, and bribery.[7] On the other hand, those who believe that order is maintained through adherence to common standards will look for the instances in which people appear to obey rules on their own volition.[8] They will weave their responses to their questions around the facts that they have gathered in the net of their initial concepts. Similarly, those interested in the problem of freedom will look for facts that will support solutions to this problem. Rather than focusing attention on how people come to behave in predictable patterns, they are concerned with how people surmount obstacles to self-determination.[9] This conceptual searchlight casts a beam over a different set of facts than the set revealed by the problem of order. For example, rather than force, fraud, bribery, or rote learning, those concerned with the problem of freedom tend to look at the dynamics of criticism; how people can burst through the structures of myth in which they are often enveloped.[10] For those seeking solutions to the problem of order, the process of criticism, or self-examination, might not even appear to be a fact. Some of these thinkers seem to be unaware that such a process occurs. On the other hand, those seeking solutions to the problem of freedom may tend to minimize or even ignore the role of such factors as bribery (subtle and overt) or of praise and blame in determining behavior. They will just not "see" these processes taking place, and may reduce the human drama to an interplay between force and freedom.[11]

Processes of Assimilating Facts The preceding discussion should make it clear that human beings are not born with the capability of knowing the facts. Although none of us knows what it is like to be a newborn infant, it is probable that experience is originally a humming and buzzing confusion.[12] The infant does not distinguish himself from the world and others until adult human beings initiate a process of learning.[13] As the child grows up he learns how to carve up his experience into slices and to tag those slices with names supplied by language. Names, or words, can be detached from particular experiences and carried over to new ones that are similar in certain respects. When it appears that a set of names is appropriate to a given experience, the person who makes that judgment claims that he has observed or discovered a fact. This interpretation can be disputed by someone else, who applies a different set of names to what he calls the same experience. For example, two witnesses to a murder may differ on the description of the killer. One may say the killer is a light-skinned, blue-eyed individual, and the other may say the killer is a swarthy, brown-eyed person. Neither of the witnesses, however, could have observed the "fact" had they not learned how to carve up the flux of experience into slices through the use of language.

The realization that facts do not appear in human experience apart from language should not lead to extreme skepticism and despair about one's ability to interpret experience. Rather, it should put one on guard against too ready acceptance of the "facts" in any particular case. The first reason that it is wise to be on guard is that without the aid of intelligence, the human senses are quite unreliable. They are mainly unreliable because of prejudices and predispositions that people carry with them into situations. A prejudice against dark-skinned individuals might lead someone to see a killer as someone with a dark skin even if the killer was light-skinned.[14] The second reason why it is wise to maintain a healthy skepticism is that particular sets of names are intertwined with each judgment of fact. The Marxist tends to see conflict everywhere in social life, while the pluralist tends to see competition and basic agreement. When somebody states the "facts" about a particular social situation, such as a strike or a family quarrel, it is wise to check out his vision of the human condition, if this is possible, and see if this influences his judgment.

One of the most common devices of propaganda and advertising is to play on the naive belief in "just the facts." The propagandist or mass manipulator who can convince his audience that there are pure facts apart from concepts, frameworks, theories, prejudices, predispositions, opinions, and visions has won much more than half his battle. The reason why he tends to cultivate the belief in pure facts should be clear by now. If people believe that there are facts apart from interpretations, then it becomes possible to play on prejudices that they are not always aware of. The cards can be stacked by building such assumptions into the propaganda as "the underdog is always right," "whites should feel guilty about the past slavery of blacks," "women are primarily creatures of emotion," and many other "principles" that may appear absurd when examined systematically. These assumptions are never stated outright, but lurk right beneath the surface of so-called factual reports. Also, if one believes that there are pure facts, there is no need to examine the vision of the human condition held by the propagandist. For example, a propagandist concerned with damaging the reputation of a government that has come to power through revolution may sketch a portrait of the revolution in which the execution of the members of the old ruling class, the disruption of everyday life and the dictatorial methods of the new governers are stressed. The image of the human condition underlying this portrait may be that revolutions are always greater evils than whatever preceded them, and that forms of government should only be changed peacefully.[15] Thus, the propagandist selects "facts" to fit his underlying image of the human condition without ever informing his audience about that image. Of course, he leaves out those "facts" that would tend to cast doubt on the accuracy of his image, such as reports of the abuses of the old regime, the low standard of living and extreme inequalities of wealth that were present in the past, and the failure of the old ruling class to respond to peaceful movements for improvement. The propagandist hopes that his audience will accept his portrait of the horrors of the revolution as the relatively complete description of the "facts of the case" and that they will not look any farther for other facts or for his underlying image of the human condition.

Separating Facts from Opinion Holding the belief that it is possible to get "just the facts" without an overlay of interpretation makes one an easy mark for propaganda and shows that one has little respect for his thought processes. The scientific attitude toward studying the human condition goes in the very opposite direction from asking immediately for the facts. The first step in scientific investigation is to make sure of the question that one is asking. Suppose that one is asking the question: Should the federal government support day-care centers for the children of working mothers?[16] Before this question can be answered yes or no, it must be analyzed and clarified. First, it is necessary to understand what is meant by the term "should." Usually, it refers to urging adoption of those actions that are required to realize a vision of the good society held by the person who is using the term. So, the first step that must be taken is not to get any facts, but to see whether or not day-care centers are part of one's vision of the good society. If it turns out that they are, the next question is whether or not the federal government is the proper agency to support day-care centers. The word "proper" here usually means: Will federal funding be an efficient means to the end of day-care centers without blocking the realization of other aspects of the good society? Alternative answers to this question will be debated fiercely by opposing sides. Those in favor of day-care centers will point to the successes of the federal government as an agent in supporting programs, while those opposed to them will point to failures. Both sides will be drawing upon "facts" to support their cases. In order to interpret these "facts" it is necessary to have a standard of what makes for success and failure. This is not a factual judgment either. Those opposed to day-care centers will try to show that every deviation from some ideal of a perfect government program is a dismal failure, while those in favor of them will try to show that slight improvements over past conditions are glowing successes. One must decide what he means by success. Only after this is done is it time to look at the "facts" and, perhaps, for them. In this case, the facts will be examples of similar programs that have been attempted in the past and a determination of their results. All of those results will not be investigated; only those consequences that bear on the definition of success and failure that has been chosen. Thus, the "facts" follow the framework supplied by the questions. Out of the enormous complexity of human events, the questions that one asks illuminate slices of activity and identify them as facts.[17]

Once a person has a good idea of the facts that he is seeking, the accuracy of these facts becomes extremely important. This is why in the natural sciences and in some parts of sociology the development of means of accurate measurement is considered a central aspect of investigation. The significance of accuracy can be illustrated by following the example of day-care centers further. Suppose that one has decided to find out whether or not federally supported programs similar to a possible program of day-care centers have been successful. The major task now is to identify the results of these programs. These results will be framed by such questions as whether or not the federal monies got spent on the people who were supposed to benefit from them, whether the projected benefits actually accrued, and whether there were unintended consequences, favorable and not, of the federal support. There are many ways of attempting to gain answers to such questions, some of which will be discussed in the next chapter. However, what is important at this point is to note that, in the absence of factual accuracy, one will not be able to make an intelligent decision about the desirability of federal funding for day-care centers. Accuracy will be judged according to certain standards set up within the methods of determining "facts." Each method will have its own standards for determining what kinds of observations are fit to enter the realm of fact. Some methods will consider as fact what appears in official documents, firsthand reports, travelogues, newspaper and magazine articles, and other such sources. Other methods will consider as fact what is personally observed by the investigator after he has familiarized himself directly with the human activity he is studying. Still other methods will state that facts are what appear in census reports, while others will claim that facts are found in responses to questionnaires. Finally, some methods will admit as full scientific facts only those activities observed under experimentally controlled conditions. Whatever the standards, of course, the sociologist will attempt to be as accurate as possible according to those standards.

Scientific Inquiry and Fact Finding The interest of scientists in factual accuracy is another way that they are distinguished from propagandists and advertisers. The scientist is often more concerned with the ways in which the facts were arrived at (their grounds) than with their content. If the "facts" merely represent wishful thinking on someone's part they are worthless from the scientist's viewpoint, unless he happens to be studying wishful thinking. On the other hand, the propagandist will use any facts that he can get hold of that appear to support his case. If he becomes concerned with accuracy it will not be because he is interested in furthering inquiry into the object of study, but because he is afraid if he becomes too inaccurate his opponents will expose him and he will lose effectiveness. Thus, the very propagandist who claims to offer "just the facts" is often engaging in as much distortion and outright fraud as he can get away with. At the same time, the scientist who is doubtful about ever reaching a point where he knows "just the facts" is engaged in a quest for accuracy.

This seeming paradox reveals something very important about scientific inquiry and the entire process of self-examination. Science begins with doubt rather than certainty, questions rather than answers, problems rather than solutions.[18] It does not rest with quick answers based upon wishful thinking, but it also does not remain in a mass of confusion and extreme skepticism. Rather, it attempts to disclose the principles of clear thinking and then apply them to the investigation of experience. When one applies these principles to the study of human activity, one is a sociologist. A statement of fact is an answer to the question, What happened? The scientist knows the obstacles in the way of answering that question and attempts to perfect methods for surmounting these obstacles. The propagandist merely attempts to cook up an answer which will serve his purposes and gain the belief of people who think that there are facts without interpretations.

EXERCISE

Listen to an advertisement on TV for a product you have used. Then determine which facts were used in the advertisement and attempt to discover the underlying image of the product the commercial seeks to convey. What facts about the product could you organize to give a different image from the one in the advertisement?

EXERCISE

Listen to or read about a debate on some political issue (for example, the Arab-Israeli conflict). Determine which facts are considered important by each side and then reconstruct the image each side has of the conflict. Which "facts" do the two images have in common? Which "facts" are included by one side and not the other?

PRECISION

Closely related to factual accuracy is precision. Precision has to do with the way in which ideas relate to observations. Suppose that someone says that "India and Pakistan have fought a war." This is a factual statement. However, before we know whether to judge this statement true or false, we must determine the meaning of the term "war." Does this term allow us to distinguish precisely between one kind of event and others? Perhaps the person who made the statement meant that war is "what happens when two groups or individuals do not like each other." This would be an imprecise or vague definition, because it is quite difficult to determine when two nations do not like each other. When does indifference end and disliking begin? What about mixed emotions? Do groups have feelings in the first place and, if they do, how are these feelings expressed? These are the kinds of questions that appear when social thinking is founded on vague ideas, rather than on precise relations between ideas and observations. Due to a healthy skepticism about facts, scientists attempt to maximize precision in their observations. They attempt to approach a situation in which any human being who understood the definition that they were using would reach the same decision about identifying a particular case as anyone else using that definition.[19] With this in mind, one sociologist has defined war as "armed extensive conflict between organized bodies of people, regarding themselves as politically sovereign and ethically entitled to assert by force their rights, which they claim to be blocked or invaded by their armed opponents."[20] This definition makes it far easier to determine whether or not there is a "war" going on than the definition of war as "what happens when two groups or individuals do not like each other."

Does the preceding discussion mean that one definition of war is "better" than the other? Is the definition given by the sociologist the "real" definition of war? What if one does not like this sociologist's definition of war because it does not include such events as "wars" between teenage gangs and bands of organized criminals? These questions lead to the conclusion that, until other information is provided, the sociologist's definition of war is better than the other only in the sense that it is more precise. One could define "war" as the number of clams in Mrs. Murphy's chowder. This would be a precise definition, but it might not be altogether adequate.

The Importance of Definitions A definition identifies a slice of experience and attaches a name to it. This means that no definition is more "real" than any other. If someone defines "war" as the number of clams in Mrs. Murphy's chowder it is not enough to answer that he has not "really" defined war. What could the word "really" mean in this case? It could only mean that experience comes to human beings as a set of pigeon holes that put everything in place and leave a place for everything. This would mean that education is a process of learning to pigeonhole everything in its proper place. Once a person had mastered the great filing system of the mind, he could sit back with a contented smile on his face with the knowledge that nothing in the world could ever disturb him again, because he would know where to file every future experience. For someone who adopts this view of experience, the present book is useless. The present book is based upon the idea that experience is a continually shifting and dynamic process with many facets. According to this perspective, there are no "real" definitions because language is like a net cast over experience with the purpose of catching certain slices or phases of this experience and holding them for future reference. "In the beginning was the word" because, without the word, experience would be merely a formless and chaotic flux.[21]

Although there are no "real" definitions, some definitions are better than others, in the sense that they are well adapted to the solution of particular problems or to the attainment of particular goals. If the goal is understanding what happened between India and Pakistan, defining war as the number of clams in Mrs. Murphy's chowder is not as useful as defining war in some more traditional way. It is only after the purpose of inquiry has been defined that the standard of precision can be applied meaningfully to definitions. Thus, if the purpose is to describe what happens between teen-age gangs when they come into conflict, it may be quite useful to define the term "war" to include these events.

Propaganda and Precision When it comes to precision, propagandists work in the very opposite way from scientists. They are usually imprecise and they also attempt to make people believe that there are "real" definitions of happenings. One staple of propaganda is to stretch the ordinary meaning of words to include new events. The aim is to have the audience associate the event with the emotion that normally accompanies the word. For example, when people raise their voices during a demonstration, administrators say that their words are "violent." This stretches the ordinary meaning of violence to include loud voices, and has the aim of turning opinion against the demonstrators. Another staple of propaganda is to narrow the ordinary meaning of words to exclude new events. For example, when administrators call in police to break up demonstrations and the police begin clubbing the demonstrators, the administrators may state that clubbing is not "violence" but "self-defense."[22] This narrows the ordinary meaning of violence to exclude the use of force by police, and has the aim of turning opinion in favor of the police and the administrators. In such cases, the underlying definition of violence seems to be "any activity the administrators do not like." This is quite an imprecise definition and does not allow people to hold particular slices of experience for future reference.

Propagandists also attempt to convince people that certain definitions are more "real" than others. Such attempts are usually made when the propagandist is trying to use words that have highly favorable emotional associations attached to them. For example, suppose a group of Christians such as the Campus Crusade for Christ or the Jesus People is attempting to convert radical students to their creed. They will claim that Christianity is truly "revolutionary" whereas demonstrations are not "really" revolutionary. On the other hand, such radical groups as the SDS will claim that they are the authentic revolutionaries while the Jesus People are "really" reactionaries. Both groups believe that the people they are trying to convert have favorable emotional associations with the term "revolution." Thus, instead of trying to convince people to join them by telling them what kind of experiences they can expect if they enter the given movement, they try to induce people to join them by throwing around words with favorable emotional associations. Perhaps this means that they believe that people would never join up if they knew what they were in for.[23]

Some people have been so disturbed by such propaganda tactics that they have suggested that only the precise use of ordinary language will prevent the domination of the mind by power groups.[24] This position is understandable in the light of the abuses noted above, but in the long run it is unsound. If experience is dynamic, then shifting and multidimensional ordinary language must change along with it if it is to express the new possibilities seen by free human beings. Such change demands experimentation and a relatively large measure of imprecision.

EXERCISE

Listen to or read a political speech or an advertisement. Were there any terms used so imprecisely that you could interpret the statement in more than one way? If so, determine what purposes the imprecision might serve.

CONSISTENCY AND COHERENCE

In the discussion of precision we noted the tendency of propagandists to expand and narrow the definitions of terms to suit their particular purposes. What would be called violence if done by the opposition would be called peaceful advocacy if done by the propagandist's allies. What would be called self-defense if done by the propagandist's allies would be called violence if done by the opposition. In the first case the definition of violence is expanded to include shouting. In the second case it is contracted to exclude the use of force by one's allies. This shifting of definitions should not be confused with inconsistency. When definitions are shifted, the same word is used to mean more than one thing. When definitions are inconsistent or contradictory, they both affirm and deny the same thing.

A contradictory claim is a claim that a statement and its negation are both true. An example of a contradictory definition is, "War is what happens when two groups dislike one another and not what happens when two groups dislike one another." An example of a contradictory claim is, "India and Pakistan fought a war, and India and Pakistan did not fight a war." It is clear that war cannot be both what happens when two groups dislike one another and not what happens when they dislike one another. It is clear that India and Pakistan could not both fight a war and not fight a war. It is important to note that war could be defined as what happens when two groups dislike one another or not what happens when two groups dislike one another. In this case the term "war" would be a synonym for the word "everything." Similarly, one could truthfully claim that either India and Pakistan fought a war or India and Pakistan did not fight a war, though it might take some figuring out to determine why a person would make such a statement.

Scientists attempt to avoid contradiction in both their definitions and their claims. Given the examples above, this would seem to be an easy task. However, in difficult and complex studies contradictions often creep in, thereby rendering much of the work nonsense. For example, someone may claim that human beings seek pleasure and avoid pain. Discussion may proceed for a time on this basis until someone else asks, "What about masochists who seek to be hurt?" Perhaps the response will be, "Well, for that kind of person pain *is* pleasure." Is this response contradictory to the original statement that human beings seek pleasure and avoid pain? A yes-or-no answer to this question is impossible until definitions are checked. If by the term pleasure the person means "that which is sought by people" and by pain he means "that which is not sought by people" he is not in contradiction, for he has simply been arguing that people seek what they seek and avoid what they avoid. This kind of argument is tautological, or true by definition. If, however, by the term pleasure the person means a specific feeling and by pain a different feeling, then he is in contradiction.

Scientists attempt to avoid contradiction because they aim at accurate and systematic description of experience. Propagandists will attempt to employ contradiction whenever they believe it will serve the interests that they are trying to promote. For example, some religious promoters will define God as a supreme Person ruling the universe and then state that every person seeks God. If confronted by a person who claims that he does not believe in God nor seek God, the promoter will ask, "Well, do you seek anything?" The person may answer, "Yes, I seek social justice." Then the religious promoter will respond, "Well now, social justice is your God and so you do seek God after all." This kind of argument is contradictory, because the religious promoter will not usually admit that he means by God anything that human beings seek. However, though the propaganda is contradictory, it is sometimes successful in converting unsuspecting souls.

Even more serious than actual contradiction is the tendency of much propaganda to undermine the standard of consistency itself. Matching the misguided quest for "just the facts" are such phrases as "foolish consistency," "cold and unfeeling reason," and "life is larger than logic." When people use such phrases it means that either they want to avoid undertaking the task of self-understanding or that they want to prevent others from undertaking this task. It is obvious that if people can be persuaded that maintaining consistency is foolish, heartless, or stupid they will tend not to look seriously upon contradictions when they appear in propaganda. This does not mean that a person should never change his plans or intentions. There is nothing contradictory about planning to become an engineer and later deciding to become a sociologist, or vice versa, as long as one realizes that a plan has been changed. There is also nothing cold and unfeeling, or dead, about attempting to be consistent. In fact, the attempt to fashion a consistent image of the human condition can be one of the most exciting adventures in thought, because the very points where contradictions are detected are usually the points where one is most resistant to change and most self-protective.[25] A very good way of understanding oneself or another thinker is to track down the contradictions. They will appear at the points where a person is unwilling to surrender a principle even though it is confronted with a sharp challenge. Examples of such principles are the ideas that all people seek pleasure and avoid pain or that God is a supreme Person ruling the universe who everybody seeks. Since scientists aim at accurate and systematic description of experience, they are willing to surrender or alter principles when they stand in the way of attaining this aim. Since the science of human affairs is the process of self-understanding and clarification, everyone who would seek self-understanding must be scientific in the sense of trying to avoid contradiction.

EXERCISE

You are probably familiar with the views on society and social relations held by one or both of your parents. Are there any contradictions or inconsistencies in these views? (For example, do your parents proclaim a belief in equality and then say that you can only date people from certain groups?) If you can find any inconsistencies, can you account for them by some motive of self-protection? Can you account for them in any other ways?

A good indication of the importance of consistency in human existence is that a familiar way of dominating people is to make them and others believe that they are incapable of consistency. Thus, racist snobs have spread the belief that blacks are incapable of reasoned thought, and some people in the middle class have spread the belief that working people are incapable of reasoned thought.[26] A very large number of people believe that old people naturally become "senile" and, therefore, incapable of reason. Another large number of people believe that women are "basically" creatures of emotion. Many women seem to like this idea and claim a right to be inconsistent. In accepting this badge of inferiority they are playing a cheap trick on themselves and on other women in an attempt to be cute and win concessions in a fundamentally unequal relationship. As was pointed out in the first chapter, the greatest barrier to self-understanding is contempt for the mind. The invariable result of such contempt is exploitation.

Closely related to the standard of consistency is the standard of coherence. A coherent description is one in which the names used in describing the events exhaust the subject, are about the same thing, and do not overlap one another. For example, suppose that one was describing families and divided them into families containing more than one married pair and their offspring (extended families) and families containing no more than one married pair and their offspring (nuclear families). These categories would not overlap, would exhaust the subject, and would be about the same thing. Suppose the category of nuclear family was dropped from the system of classification and in its place was substituted the category of "happy family." Now the categories would overlap, would not exhaust the subject, and would be about different things. They would overlap because some extended families might also be happy. They would not exhaust the subject because some families with no more than one married pair might be unhappy. They would not be about the same thing since one category would define families according to happiness and the other category would define families according to the number of married pairs contained.

Scientists seek coherence in their descriptions of experience. It is only with a coherent system of names that facts can be accurately identified. Imagine a person doing research on the family with only the categories *extended family* and *happy family* available to him. Imagine further that this researcher could classify each family he observed in only one of the two categories. Where would he put the *happy extended family*? Where would he put the *unhappy nuclear family*? Coherence, of course, is not prized by the propagandist. In fact, he thrives on incoherence. For example, a popular form of propaganda is the statement that there are only two kinds of societies in the present world—i.e., capitalist democracies and communist dictatorships. Someone who accepts this classification system has a hard time classifying a capitalist dictatorship, a communist democracy, or some other form of society such as a socialist democracy. Usually the propagandist wants the individual to believe that all capitalist societies are democracies and all communist societies are dictatorships. Thus, he wants to cloak capitalism in the garments of democracy. This example shows how important it is to inspect carefully the coherence of one's categories. Without a coherent set of names many significant experiences will be lost to awareness and others will be hopelessly distorted.

ADEQUACY

Suppose that a person worked up a vision of the human condition that was factually accurate, precise, consistent, and coherent. Suppose further that another individual also worked up such a vision, but that it was different. How would someone be able to judge between these two visions? Both would meet the formal standards of science perfectly, but both would select out of human experience different facts and different categories. The first impulse might be to say that, as long as both visions are accurate and consistent, the choice among them is simply a matter of taste. That it is possible to take this position is proven by its popularity in the contemporary world. However, it is worthwhile to attempt to find out whether one can do any better than arbitrary whim.

One way of going beyond mere taste is to argue that the task of science is to explain the events that occur in experience. The general form of explanation is by a law linking two kinds of events together in time. An example of a law is that the volume of a gas increases in direct proportion to the amount of heat. This law allows one to explain particular cases of gases expanding in volume, as well as to predict when and how the volume of gases will expand in the future.

For most of its history, sociology has been a search for laws of human activity. Up until this time, few if any laws have been discovered. Despite, however, the lack of success on this score, the majority of sociologists continue to claim that their efforts are justified by the future possibility of a set of interrelated laws of human activity.[27] Sociologists point to physical science as an example of what they might accomplish. They are particularly impressed by two features of physical science. First, the physical sciences contain an interrelated body of generalizations that describe the succession of events accurately enough to be used for prediction of future events. This is the element of law in physical science. Second, the laws in physical science are derived logically from a small set of axioms. These axioms present a model of physical motion. Many sociologists hope for a future science of human activity that would be logically derived from a small set of axioms presenting a model of human behavior. In such a science of human activity, all the various generalizations about behavior would be tied together by this model. If sociologists have been thus far unsuccessful in discovering laws of human activity, they have been doubly unsuccessful in relating the tendencies that they have observed to a model of human behavior contained in a small set of axioms.

It is not our intention to question the presence of regularities and tendencies in human affairs. Without such regularities and tendencies human existence would be a mere chaos and we could not be even writing this book with the expectation that it could be read and understood. Thus, the search for trends, tendencies, and other regularized successions, even if it does not end in the discovery of universal laws, should be encouraged by those seeking self-understanding. Accurate description of such tendencies is of great help in supporting or casting doubt upon particular visions of the human condition. For example, suppose a person is organizing a vision of the human condition around the relations between men and women, and claims that the growing number of divorces is due to the fact that women have begun doing "men's work." The validity of this vision would be in doubt if it was found that the divorce rate was lower in marriages where the wife was doing work traditionally restricted to males than in other marriages. One need not adopt a physical science model of the human sciences to affirm that statements about regularized successions in human affairs should be substantiated.

While substantiated generalizations are valuable to a human science, the attempt to devise a small set of axioms about human behavior from which these generalizations could be logically derived contradicts the very principles upon which this book is based. The process of clarification, generalization, relativization, and commitment is a process of freedom. It is based on the premises that human beings can keep part of their experience detached from immediate social requirements, can say no to commands, can choose among alternatives, and can create new alternatives. It is this process that defines human existence rather than some axiom like "men seek pleasure and avoid pain." One begins work in the human sciences either with the principle of freedom or the principle of determinism. If one accepts the principle of determinism, one will seek a small set of axioms from which all human behavior can be derived. If one adopts the principle of freedom one will see the human sciences as opportunities to expand awareness of one's situation.

Adequacy: A Standard for Evaluation If one adopts the principle of freedom, it becomes necessary to supply an alternative standard to logical derivation from a small set of axioms for evaluating images of the human condition. Such a standard can be called "adequacy." By adequacy is meant the degree to which the vision makes sense of one's situation by knitting the various parts of it into a meaningful whole. This is not the same as evaluating thought according to whether one "likes" it or not. One may like an image of the human condition which ignores such experiences as death, exploitation, and war, but such an image will not be adequate because it is not comprehensive enough to take account of these factors. Further, the judgment of adequacy only makes sense when applied to visions that tend toward factual accuracy, precision, consistency, and coherence. However, there is an element of "insight" in judgments of adequacy that is not reducible to the formal standards of science or to comprehensiveness. This kind of insight is similar to the appreciation of painting. In painting, the artist organizes parts of the visual field. He selects out certain colors and forms, and leaves out others. He puts some colors and forms in the foreground and others in the background. A similar process takes place in creating images of the human condition. The human scientist selects certain experiences such as economic production or religious activity to compose his vision, and he leaves out others. Given his selection from the whole mass of human activity, he places stress on these features in an order of significance. The result is an image into which the reader or listener can imaginatively enter and find a place for himself. For example, if Marxism is considered in this way, the individual enters into the image as the member of some economic class and is able to appreciate his situation with respect to others in a new way. By doing this he has gained an insight into the relation of his activity to the wider activities going on around him.

What does the term significance mean with respect to visions of the human condition? It is a judgment of what that image means for one's entire existence as a human being. Some images are grotesque in the sense that they appear to distort human existence even if they are relatively accurate and consistent. For example, we find the vision of the human condition presented by prohibitionists to be grotesque. It is difficult for us to make sense out of our lives by organizing all our experiences around the supposed evils of consuming alcoholic beverages. The same goes for visions of the human condition organized around the benefits of eating "organic" foods or of taking consciousness-expanding drugs. Yet some people find these visions, or others like them, to be more than adequate. From these differences in judgment we do not draw the conclusion that "beauty is in the eye of the beholder" or that "it is all a matter of taste." There will always be differences in vision, but some people arrive at their visions through rigorously undertaking the process of self-understanding, while others arrive at their visions somewhat impulsively. For us, it is this process that makes all the difference, because we are not so vain as to believe that our vision of the contemporary world is the most adequate one.

It is merely the most adequate one that we have been able to develop over time and through efforts at self-understanding.

Adequacy can be judged to some extent by the richness of a vision and its plausibility. One vision is richer than another when it provides a greater number of reasons why people might relate to one another in certain ways. For example, an account of conflict between ethnic groups which included motivations and reasons drawn from economic competition, power relations, religious rivalry, and language difference would be richer than one employing only language difference. A vision is more plausible than another when, through using imagination, one can make sense of the reasons given for a social relation in terms of one's own actual and possible experience. Plausibility is far less precise a standard than richness and should be used with care. One may find an account of human existence implausible merely because of one's own narrow experience or the limitations of one's imagination.

There is a way of making plausibility somewhat more precise—a kind of standard that one can use to approach a measure of adequacy. Suppose that two competing visions of the human condition are to be judged; suppose further that the advocate of one of these visions has understood only the image he favors, while the advocate of the other vision has understood both images. One would tend to trust the judgment of the person who had understood both images rather than that of the person who had understood only one.[28] This standard, of course, is merely a rough measure, because it is very difficult to judge whether or not one understands a vision of the human condition in its most important implications. The standard is most useful in picking out those who are making no effort at wider understanding, but who instead resist the process of self-understanding and prefer to rest content with whatever prejudices they happen to have. Ultimately, adequacy can be tested only through insight.[29] It should be obvious by now, however, that if insight is to be valuable it must be hedged by high intellectual standards such as factual accuracy, precision, consistency, coherence, and comprehensiveness, as well as by active commitment to the process of self-understanding. It is the use of such standards that distinguishes insight from taste. Perhaps the most important difference between the human sciences and propaganda is that the propagandist attempts to paint an image of the human condition based on wishful thinking, while the human scientist attempts to construct a vision based on accurate description of experience. Wishful thinking is the philosophy of the playpen and, unfortunately, of the board rooms of many corporation directors, military leaders, political bosses, and university trustees. From our perspective, the mark of maturity is the application of science to one's own life. Propagandists attempt to convince people that science is rigorous, dull and painful. They try to make them believe that to be scientific means that one turns into a robot or a human computer. Nothing could be further from the truth. While there is no doubt that science is rigorous, the rigors of a human science are both exciting and enjoyable.

FRUITFULNESS

A human science is not merely a description of human activity, but also an invitation to action. There is no sharp distinction between thought and action in human existence—one must act to gain knowledge. Thus, the methods discussed in the next chapter are really modes of action. One uses knowledge in acting. Within one's everyday activity are displayed certain assumptions about human relations that constitute an active vision of the human condition. This means that, when one clarifies his image of the human condition, certain modes of action seem more reasonable to undertake than others. For example, the prohibitionist will be directed toward action aimed at ending the manufacture and sale of alcoholic beverages, while the Marxist will be oriented toward action aimed at changing the system by which the means of production are owned and controlled. Each vision of the human condition situates the person in a wider domain of action, points out likely allies and opponents, and suggests measures to be taken for altering or preserving human relations.

The fact that each image of the human condition suggests courses of action leads to judging these images on the basis of their fruitfulness for action. While the physical sciences provide predictions, the human sciences provide possibilities. The physical scientist will predict that if a gas is heated its volume will expand. The human scientist will offer the possibility of, for example, changing the ownership and control of the means of production through revolution. There will be alternative possibilities to that one, elements of choice will enter, and future human beings will experience them. Thus, the possibilities provided by visions of the human condition are really invitations to living experimentation with human existence. This judgment leads to the question of whether there is any standard according to which possibilities should be chosen. This is a moral question, and an answer to it is implied in all of the preceding discussion. Visions of the human condition should not be judged merely according to the quantity of possibilities they reveal for action, but according to whether these possibilities promise to extend and reinforce the process of self-understanding.[30] Thus, the most fruitful images of the human condition will be those that provide the most possibilities for expanding clarification, generalization, relativization and commitment. This judgment is inescapable once one has adopted a human science based on freedom rather than determinism.

Much propaganda runs counter to a human science with regard to orientation towards the future. Some propagandists make believe that the possibilities they offer are predictions. They say that people have a "chance not a choice" to join the inevitable revolutionary movement or whatever other movement they are promoting.[31] Other propagandists tell people that they are already "free" and that they have no obligation to undertake the process of self-understanding. Both kinds of propaganda are attempts to bring the future under control through manipulating human beings. The "chance not a choice" appeal is an attempt to make people believe that they have no control over their own destinies, but that they are pawns of "history." The appeal to irresponsible "freedom" is an attempt to convince people to stay just the way they are so that they can remain easy pickings for existing power groups. Thus, the propagandist is ultimately out to make people into either mindless fanatics obeying the directions of a leadership group, or else grasping children manipulated by advertising and public relations technicians. The first technique is primarily used by the totalitarian political movement, while the second is mainly used by the conglomerate organizations of the West.

Figure 3.1. STANDARDS FOR EVALUATING A VISION OF THE HUMAN CONDITION

Natural Science Model	Human Science Model
1. Factual Accuracy	1. Factual Accuracy
2. Precision	2. Precision
3. Consistency and Coherence	3. Consistency and Coherence
4. Explanation (Under what conditions do specific events appear?)	4. Adequacy (Do diverse events fall into a plausible context?)
5. Prediction (Under what conditions will specific events appear?)	5. Fruitfulness (Does the image reveal new possibilities for action?

EXERCISE

What kind of image of the human condition would be most appropriate for getting people to obey a leader blindly?

What kind of image of the human condition would be most appropriate for encouraging people to act freely?

What kind of image of the human condition would be most appropriate for discouraging action?

Devise or find images of the human condition that would mobilize masses of people to follow a program of action, that would encourage them to reach independent commitments and that would discourage them from acting politically.

HUMAN SCIENCE

Sociology is the science of the human condition. As a human science it incorporates standards for judging its own products. These standards fall into four general categories—factual accuracy, consistency, adequacy, and fruitfulness.

A factual judgment is an answer to the question: Did it happen? There are no such things as pure "facts" separated from some framework of interpretation and some procedures for observing experience. Scientists attempt to make clear the frameworks guiding their search for facts and the procedures they are using to gather them. Propagandists pretend that their messages communicate the bare facts of the case.

Consistency is the avoidance of contradiction. Scientists aim for consistency in their descriptions by attempting to avoid saying that the same statement is both true and false. Propagandists will be inconsistent when they believe that it will serve their aims and that they will be able to get away with it.

Adequacy is the quality of an image of the human condition that allows it to make sense out of the various aspects of human activity. Human scientists aim for adequacy by attempting to paint an image of the human condition that is comprehensive, significant and grounded in consistent reports of fact. Propagandists aim for adequacy by appeal to wishful thinking.

Fruitfulness refers to the possibilities for action revealed by a vision of the human condition. Human scientists aim for a fruitfulness that will expand the process of self-understanding. Propagandists attempt to convince people that they should obey the orders of some elite group or that they should stay the way they are.

The practice of human science within everyday existence demands adherence to the standards of accuracy, consistency, adequacy, and fruitfulness. Adherence to these standards demands both respect for one's mind and knowledge of the methods of inquiry that are used to gain knowledge about the human condition. Gaining confidence in one's mind requires overcoming the barriers to self-understanding discussed in the first chapter. The methods of gaining knowledge about the human condition are discussed in the next chapter.

4

METHOD WITHOUT MADNESS

How does one arrive at a fairly complete vision of the human condition? Most people pick up information from their families and friends, and from the mass media such as radio, television, and newspapers. Along with this information come built-in interpretations and, without too much awareness, most people adopt a mixture of these interpretations as their image of the human condition.

Much of what is presented as news on the evening newscast can be seen as attempts to portray the human condition. Astronauts' wives are stoic and prayerful as their husbands fly through space; neighbors of a tragedy-stricken family are quick to rally and give aid; parents try to block the busing of their children aimed at achieving integration; people flock to football stadiums in frigid weather but tend to avoid voting if drizzles are predicted for election day; the President says that we all must sacrifice for the public good; the struggle for women's equality involves integrating bars and becoming jockeys. . . . Critics of the mass media claim that the human condition presented through them is partial and distorted, and meant to make people favor the status quo. William Ernest Hocking wrote that most people today gain their images of the human condition from "accepted moulders of crowd opinion," like propagandists, advertisers, and public relations men.[1]

The partiality, distortions, and prepackaged interpretations built into the most available sources of information about the public situation make it necessary for those in search of self-understanding to push beyond these sources. It also becomes necessary to use more active and reliable methods than merely watching the evening news to gather and interpret information. Since generalization, relativization, and, ultimately, commitment are based upon beliefs, the quality and type of information about the human condition are very important. The procedures used to gather this information are generally referred to as methods. Thus, method is a series of regularized acts pursued to gain previously unknown knowledge. The specific content of the knowledge is, of course, not known (documenting the obvious is a pointless activity), but the means of gaining the knowledge are fully in awareness.

In some ways, using a method is like fishing. Putting a baited hook on a string, attaching it to a pole to extend it further, dropping it into the water and retrieving it when a tugging is felt are all procedures in a method for catching fish. Where and when one fishes and the type of hook, line, bait, and rod one uses depend upon the variety of fish one is after. Although the method is known, the goal is at best only partly known. The method may be specific to a given species of fish, but the particular fish, or even the size or weight, cannot be specified in advance. In sociology, as in fishing, one chooses a method to suit one's goal. We do not need a sophisticated angler to tell us that we will not catch a barracuda by dropping a worm on a safety pin tied to a string into a pond. Likewise in sociology, certain methods are more appropriate for gaining some kinds of knowledge than are others. For example, one would hardly use a self-administered questionnaire to find out from which social groupings suicides come.

The analogy between sociological methods and fishing breaks down, however, because fishing is usually considered a diversion rather than an authentic activity in which the result matters. While a sportsman is not concerned ultimately with the uses to which his catch will be put, a sociologist should be concerned with the uses that are made of his findings. The sportsman will often allow his equipment to determine his goal. Sociologists, on the other hand, choose their goal, which in turn determines to some extent the method they employ. If one is a serious inquirer, a particular method is not used because it is popular or easily funded, or because the researcher is skilled in its use, but because it seems likely to help solve a problem, to give new information. To let the means determine the end is to fall prey to what Abraham Kaplan refers to as the Law of the Instrument: "Give a small boy a hammer, and he will find that everything he encounters needs pounding."[2]

Before any method is selected, the first step is to answer the question, What do I want to find out about? Responses to this question may be as varied as how many people agree with a given position, under what conditions people discriminate against others, the effects of worker self-management in factories on efficiency and job satisfaction, and what factors influence police rioting. There are, of course, a multitude of other possible responses.

A second question to ask oneself is, Why do I want to know this information? For some researchers, unfortunately, the answer is "to enable some people to manipulate others" or, more simply, "because I am being paid to find this out." For others, the goal is to reduce human behavior to a series of universal laws. A purer approach is to take neither of these two positions, and do research to make available information that will help ourselves and others clarify, generalize, and relativize images of the human condition. Such research is intended to provide fruitful possibilities for action or, in C. Wright Mills' terms, "To make private problems public."

METHOD AND PARADIGM

After deciding upon a problem that one wants to investigate, an appropriate method must be selected. In some sciences, particularly branches of physics and chemistry, there is general agreement on the problems that should be explored and, usually, general agreement on the methods that should be used. Sometimes the relation between problem and method becomes so close in these disciplines that if someone comes up with a problem that is not approachable by the approved methods, the problem is declared illegitimate rather than the methods being declared inadequate. For example, I. Velikovsky was concerned with determining the origin of the earth and, by implication, of planetary bodies in general. His thesis was that the earth was formed through catastrophic events, and to demonstrate this thesis he used ancient literature, reports of myths, and sacred books. His use of the historical method to demonstrate an astronomical thesis met with derision and harsh attacks from the leaders of professional astronomy. Professional astronomers normally use methods based on telescopic observation and other physical techniques to conduct their investigations and to decide between competing interpretations of astronomical events. Since Velikovsky's thesis could not be demonstrated by these methods, the majority of professional astronomers declared his thesis illegitimate.[3]

The astronomers could laugh and scream Velikovsky out of court (whether or not they were justified in so doing) because they agreed upon the problems that astronomers should explore and the methods that they should use. When there is such agreement on problem and method in a science, that science is said to have a *paradigm.* Thomas Kuhn in *The Structure of Scientific Revolutions* describes the process whereby a paradigm is established in a discipline and then reigns supreme. For example, Newton's paradigm of physical motion unified the science of physics for a time because it accounted for a great deal of work being done at the time on the problem of motion and showed an impressive application of mathematical technique to this problem. Almost all paradigms have emerged victorious from a battle against competitors. Thus, revolutions that attempt to install a new paradigm are sometimes successful. Unsuccessful attempts have on occasion led to the founding of new disciplines. Paradigms unify the activity of scientific inquiry through a division of scientific labor. Theorists work on the most general principles of the paradigm and attempt to make them consistent. Experimenters test the implications of the general principles to see whether or not they are factually accurate. Applied scientists devise ways in which the principles can be used in attaining human goals. In this way, a scientific "community," or discipline, forms around a paradigm. The existence of paradigms and of "scientific revolutions" should lead to the recognition that science is by no means a repository of absolute and changeless knowledge. There are always intelligent and informed people who do not accept the given paradigm of a discipline, and who carry on a continuous war with the dominant group. Some of them are reactionaries, attempting to carry on a paradigm that has been discarded by most professionals, while others are revolutionaries out to install a new paradigm. They are at the fringes of the discipline and do not accept the going division of labor. They are also an embarrassment to the dominant group, and attempts are made to discredit them and ride them out of the profession. This situation is one more reason not to worship science, but to attempt to understand it as a kind of inquiry.[4]

Sociology's Approach

Sociology has no single paradigm and, thus, has a number of different methods. This fact has been bemoaned by some and applauded by others. Among those unhappy with the situation are people who view the disciplines of the natural sciences as successful and worthy of emulation. They would like sociology to be based on a small set of axioms about human behavior and would like theorists to test these axioms for consistency, experimenters to test them for factual accuracy, and applied sociologists to use them in engineering the attainment of goals. As we pointed out in the last chapter, there is no way of wishing this kind of paradigm into existence and many good reasons (centering on the assumption of human freedom) for abandoning the quest for it.

At least for the present, sociology does not have a paradigm in Kuhn's sense of the term. Instead of paradigms there are visions of the human condition. There is a very important difference between a paradigm and such a vision. Adopting one paradigm rather than another (for example, adopting the wave theory of light rather than the particle theory of light) does not immediately change one's activity in everyday life. However, seriously adopting one vision of the human condition rather than another (for example, adopting Marxism rather than Christianity) does immediately change one's everyday activity. It is this immediate effect on action that makes it both unlikely and undesirable for sociology to have a paradigm. There is little worry that sociology will gain a paradigm in the near future. There is little consensus in the field either on the nature of what knowledge is to be sought or on the method to be used.[5] This is why we have not given a formal definition of sociology in this book. We hope that you will be satisfied to unify the field through the process of self-understanding rather than through any select list of problems and methods.

Besides those who would like sociology to have a paradigm are those who, disappointed by the many methods now in use in sociology, believe that once the proper method is found, all important questions could then be answered.[6] The very fact that so many methods abound indicates that the "right" one has not yet been discovered. Taken at its worst, the idea that there is one method that will provide the key to knowledge reminds one of Aladdin's quest for the magic words that would open the treasure-laden vaults. The process of self-understanding, which guides this book, is no such set of magic words. It will not answer all the important questions, but it will, we hope, help you to discover which questions are important.

DIVERSITY OF METHODS

Many sociologists are not only content with the diversity of methods within the field, but claim that this variety is necessary for furthering scientific inquiry. There are two arguments given to support this position. The first is that the goals sociologists seek are so diverse as to require different methods to attain them. La Piere's classic study of discrimination demonstrates this point well. La Piere sent out a letter to restaurants asking whether or not they would serve persons of Oriental descent (the study was conducted well before the passage of civil rights laws barring discrimination in public accommodations). Many restaurants replied that they would not serve persons of Oriental descent. This use of the questionnaire method, however, did not end La Piere's study. His next step was to visit the restaurants accompanied by Orientals. This use of a participant method disclosed that many of the same restaurants that had stated that they would not serve Orientals actually did serve them when they showed up.[7] La Piere's study shows that sociologists can have multiple goals. One goal could be to find out whether or not people are willing to predict their own discriminatory acts. A second goal could be to find out whether or not they actually discriminate. A third goal could be to discover whether or not predictions match actions. The first goal can be attained through a questionnaire method, the second goal can be attained through a participant method and the third goal through a combination of the first two methods.

The second argument in favor of a variety of sociological methods centers around the notion of validity, or the question, Is what has been reported by one method "the real honest-to-goodness truth"? This is not a question of whether the particular researcher has been honest and skillful, because studies using the same methods can often be repeated and can serve as a control for dishonesty and incompetence. The issue here is the object of study itself—human beings. Whereas a wooden block will slide down an inclined plane in the same way whether or not it is being watched, whether or not it has done so before, or whether or not the researcher wants it to do so, human beings can respond to given situations by altering their activities. Webb and his associates describe several ways in which the objects being studied, people, tend to react to research settings in such a way as to make the results of investigations invalid.[8] What ties these responses together is that the people do not act as they would if they were not in a research situation.

Method Without Madness

A general reaction is often referred to as the "guinea pig effect," defined as an awareness that one is on display.[9] Such an awareness frequently influences people to act in ways that they might not have acted had they not been conscious of an observer. For example, how "naturally" do people act when they are being filmed on home movies or when their conversations are being taped? A more specific reaction to being observed is role selection, where the research subject assumes a role that he considers appropriate to the situation, but which he does not assume in everyday life. For example, many people take the role of "expert" when responding to questions posed by a sociologist about which they know very little. They agree or disagree with policies that they have never heard of and praise or condemn men of whose positions and deeds they are ignorant. D. Smith has documented this tendency with respect to public affairs and has shown, in the process, how willing people are to take the role of "expert" when they are actually ignorant.[10]

A partial solution to the fact that people respond to research settings is the use of multiple methods. Instead of using one method to find something out, many sociologists urge that several different methods be used to cross-check one another. For example, in order to find out which individuals and groups are most powerful in a city, some sociologists will analyze newspapers and other documents, conduct interviews, and administer questionnaires.[11] However, while the use of more than one method to increase the validity of findings improves accuracy, it is unlikely that it eliminates the uncertainty of social research. This uncertainty is ultimately rooted in the fact that human beings are continually reshaping their situations. They make judgments upon their surroundings and then act to alter the surroundings or their responses to them. This creative activity is at a maximum when people are most free and most involved in the process of self-understanding; thus, the more people make human science a part of their lives, the less they will behave like robots whose movements can be perfectly calculated in advance. Perhaps the most ingenious way in which certain kinds of social research can be made questionable is for people to learn about the methods of research and how and why they are used. With such knowledge they are able to make a decision about whether or not to cooperate with the researcher, and the researcher may never know about that decision.

Most generally, methods of social research are complicated by the fact that both human science and human existence are changing simultaneously. In the natural sciences there is no assumption that changes in the science are due to fundamental changes in reality. Astronomers do not claim that during the Middle Ages the sun revolved around the earth and that in modern times the earth has been revolving around the sun. Instead, they assume that the earth revolved around the sun during the Middle Ages but that human science was not far enough developed to recognize this. No such assumptions about the uniformity of social existence can be made by human scientists. As human beings continually remake their existence, human scientists must alter their perspectives. The matter is complicated even further by the fact that human science is part of human existence and contributes to changing it. The historian E. H. Carr captured some of these difficulties, which are faced by all human scientists, in a striking passage: "The historian is like an observer watching a moving procession from an aeroplane; since there is no constant or ascertainable relation between the speed, height and direction of the aircraft and the movement of the procession, changing and unfamiliar perspectives are juxtaposed in rapid succession, as in a cubist picture, none of them wholly false, none wholly true."[12] The only change that should be made in Carr's description is that while he is observing the procession, the human scientist is taking notes on it, writing them up as interpretations and then throwing them down as leaflets. Those leaflets affect activity, and the human scientist becomes part of the procession.

CLASSIFICATION OF METHODS

Like patterns of social thought, methods of social research can be classified in many ways. One popular scheme classifies methods according to the degree that they incorporate precise measurement. "Hard" methods produce information that can be described in terms of mathematical symbols while "soft" methods produce information that can only be stated in terms of everyday language. Usually, those who employ this classification consider themselves "hard scientists," out to realize the dream of a science of human behavior based on a small set of axioms. Perhaps the more serious among them are less scientists than romantics like Don Quixote, forever tilting at windmills. In the process, they have gathered a tribe of Sancho Panzas around them who are along for the game.

The classification of methods used here is adapted to the aim of illuminating the process of self-understanding. Methods will be arranged according to the degree to which the researcher is involved in creating his information. Those methods that do not involve the creation of information by the human scientist are open for anyone to use. These can be applied immediately by anyone attempting to clarify his vision of the human condition. Those methods that do involve the creation of information by the human scientist are not available to most people because they are costly and often require the cooperation of organizations to be used. Even if one had the money, the cooperation can usually be bought only by a "licensed investigator" with an advanced degree in hand. For the purposes of self-understanding, methods relying on created information will be discussed mainly with the intention of informing you about their goals and uses, so that you will know about them when you encounter them. It will then be your choice whether or not you cooperate with the sociologist.

The general methods of investigation will be discussed here. They are not exhaustive of all sociological methods, but give some idea of the range of the discipline. The *historical method* is the one most available for use by people in their everyday existence. It involves the imaginative synthesis of information about the human condition which has already been gathered or created by others. The "founding fathers" of sociology, such as Karl Marx, Max Weber, and Emile Durkheim, relied heavily on the historical method.[13] They analyzed reports, past and present, about human existence, and wove the information into patterns illuminating the structure of social relations. Related to the historical method, and really a part of it, is the demographic method, in which statistical data (such as birth and death rates) gathered by official and other organizations are analyzed.

The *participant method* involves some creation of information because the human scientist is present in the group which he is studying. The aim of this method is to illuminate the structure of social relations by carefully observing what goes on in a group. While it is not possible for a person to gain entrance into every group in which he is interested, he can start using the participant method immediately in the groups to which he belongs. Related to the participant method is nonparticipant observation, in which the human scientist is present with the group he is studying, but not a part of it.

The survey method involves the researcher in asking specific questions to people about aspects of the human condition. Here the investigator is deeply involved in creating information. At the extreme, the research subjects may never have even thought about the questions they are being asked before being confronted by the interview or the questionnaire. Related to the survey method is the depth interview, in which the researcher asks open-ended and general questions to subjects in order to find out underlying attitudes about given questions.

While the survey method usually gets at specific attitudes, the depth interview plumbs the underlying perspectives supporting these attitudes.

The method of *experimental small groups* involves the greatest creation of information by the human scientist. These groups usually exist only for the purpose of social research and are manipulated and observed by the very people who have brought them together. The sociologists who do small-group research believe that, by organizing a group under controlled conditions, they will be able to discover general patterns of human behavior.

The discussion of these frequently used methods will proceed from those in which the data has not been created by the human scientist to those in which the information must be created by the human scientist.

The Historical Method

The historical method was the first one practiced by those who were identified as sociologists. All of the "Fathers of Sociology"—Comte, Marx, Spencer, Durkheim, Weber, etc.—used this method extensively. Thus, the historical method was begun by thinkers in the monist and pluralist traditions of social thought, who attempted to discover the causes of human activity in historical "forces." Natural-law thinkers were far more interested in identifying the nature of the good life through speculative reason and argumentation than they were in discovering pattern in history. For them, history was a shifting and imperfect flux masking the social ideal that could only be known through contemplation. Thus, the historical method came into use only in modern times. Its use is carried over, however, into process thought, and many recent thinkers such as Sorokin, MacIver, Veblen, Riesman, and Parsons have relied heavily upon the historical method.

The historical method is the basic sociological method. It is basic because the knowledge resulting from its use takes the form of a general picture of a society or an age, or a vision of the human condition. Before an investigator can even use one of the other methods he must have a general idea of the social context in which he is operating. He may not be fully aware of this context, but it will shape his work anyway. The aim of the historical method is to bring the social context, or the kinds of human relations and organizations in which people act, into sharp focus. For example, it is certainly possible for someone to conduct questionnaire research asking people what brand of toothpaste they use without being fully aware of his vision of the human condition. The historical sociologist would say that unless the investigator was aware that this research would only have meaning in an industrialized and capitalist economy in which consumers were interested in cleanliness (perhaps because of old religious associations that have been forgotten), the investigator would be more like an automation manipulated by social forces than a free inquirer.

The Concept of Ideal Types The historical method provides a context through the construction of ideal types.[14] In forming an ideal type, the sociologist selects out of a human situation those elements that seem to him to be the most significant, and then knits them together into a coherent description. This process is not mysterious and is, in fact, carried on by most people every day. For example, most people have an idea of "dictatorship" that they carry with them and use at the appropriate moments in conversation and thought. This notion of dictatorship does not refer to any particular government, though it may be based upon knowledge of a particular government. Also, no government may ever have existed that had all the traits present in the notion of dictatorship. Thus, an ideal type varies from observed social situations in two ways. First, it does not include as much as any particular social situation. Social situations are infinitely complex, and if a person decided to describe every aspect of only one he could not do it in ten lifetimes. Second, an ideal type contains some traits that particular cases may not contain. There might be no government with all the aspects of a complete dictatorship. It is also important to note that the term "ideal" does not mean here "desirable." One may use an ideal type of a dictatorship without believing that any dictatorships are desirable.

Some of these points can be illustrated by the ideal type of totalitarian dictatorship. A totalitarian dictatorship is usually defined as a regime in which a single party composed of an elite attempts through force and propaganda to suppress all other political movements and to bring all social groups under its centralized regulation.[15] This definition certainly does not include everything that goes on in any government, nor does any government fully show all the characteristics of the definition. Also, for most people, it does not define a desirable form of government. What use is it? The ideal type of totalitarian dictatorship has been very useful in identifying and highlighting certain tendencies in twentieth-century politics by bringing them together and fusing them in a description. By doing this it has allowed people to better orient themselves to events in the contemporary human condition. Many people who warn of totalitarian tendencies in the United States are guided in their perception of public affairs by this ideal type.

Construction of a good ideal type is artistic work. Totalitarian dictatorship could be defined as a regime in which a single party composed of an elite attempts through force and propaganda to suppress all other political movements and whose members wear the same colored shirts and smoke more cigars than the average man. The defect of this ideal type would be the mixing up of significant and trivial characteristics. However, there is no easy way to determine which characteristics of a complex social situation are significant and which ones are trivial. A serious study of history and current affairs, as well as a study of social thought, gives some guidelines for determining importance, but the genius of those who have brought the historical method to its fullest development has been in creating new and imaginative syntheses that have illuminated the context in which human action was occurring.

Frequently, practitioners of the historical method compare two or more ideal types to one another. In the nineteenth century, monists and pluralists set the context for most contemporary sociology by formulating ideal types of whole "societies." Frequently these images of societies were meant to represent "the way things used to be" and the "way things are now." These ideal types were compared to one another with respect to the different forms taken by the family, law, religion, politics, various aspects of the economy, the fine arts, and any other aspect of human existence that the thinker judged to be important. Each "society" was seen to have a distinctive kind of some basic characteristic that greatly influenced the other aspects of human existence described.

This was particularly the case for monistic thinkers who sought to describe the human condition in terms of a single primary factor. For example, Karl Marx found the crucial characteristic in the ownership of the means of production. This led to the distinction between "feudal societies" based on ownership of inherited lands, and "capitalist societies" based on the private ownership of industrial property. For Ferdinand Toennies the crucial distinction was whether the human will was based on love or on calculation.[16] Toennies felt that, in the premodern age, human relations were organized around the feelings of solidarity while in the modern age cold and calculating reason had taken over. Emile Durkheim contrasted two types of society on the basis of their social solidarity, or what held them together.[17] The first human societies were based on the sharing of common beliefs (mechanical solidarity) while more modern societies have been based on the interdependence springing from a division of labor in which men must trade products with one another in order to survive (organic solidarity).

Durkheim's ideal types have been very influential in contemporary sociology and show how a wide variety of information can be synthesized into a compelling description. In the archaic societies founded on a mechanical solidarity of uniform beliefs, people generally had similar skills and life-styles. Criminal law was basically repressive, punishing the offender for the outrage caused to society. This repression and continuous attempt to secure conformity was based on the fact that only through conformity could the society be held together. Modern society, founded on an organic solidarity of division of labor, is characterized by a diversity of skills and life-styles. Rather than being repressive, criminal law is restitutive, aiming at restoring the disturbed situation to harmony or equilibrium. The focus on restitution is necessitated because modern society survives through interdependencies of specialists. This society is likened to an organism in which the organs and tissues (lungs, heart, stomach, and so on) can only perform certain specific acts and cannot maintain themselves without the help of the other organs. Durkheim's point is that only through pooling their skills are people enabled to obtain what they "require." This analogy might lead one to conclude that, just as the various organs in their interdependence function for the ultimate good of the body, so people in their interdependence function for the ultimate good of society. This kind of analogy is quite misleading, because a society is a human process incorporating freedom rather than a living thing striving to maintain equilibrium. Further, even if society is treated like an organism, it is necessary to remember that diseased tissues do not contribute to the ultimate good of the body. Thus, if one really took the organic analogy seriously he might have to admit that just as surgery is sometimes required on the human body so may it sometimes be necessary on the body politic. It is unlikely that these implications are in the minds of propagandists and politicians like John F. Kennedy who say, "Ask not what your country can do for you; ask what you can do for your country."

The method of historical sociology results in a broad picture of a given society. Essentially it attempts to describe the human condition at a particular time and place. One may criticize such images of the human condition on the grounds that all comprehensive visions are somewhat inaccurate. In attempting to contrast different societies, similarities are frequently overlooked. For example, in criticizing Durkheim's vision, one can note that in modern times the division of labor is not total. There are roles, and skills that go along with them, that most people in a society fill, such as the general role of human being, child or parent. This criticism, of course, is aimed at extravagant claims for the self-sufficiency of the historical method, not at the proper use of the method.

A second criticism, aimed at some of those who have used the historical method, is that the possibilities for future action disclosed by some thinkers are very narrow. This narrowness seems to result from monistic theories which trace social changes to the operation of a single "force." Pluralistic and process patterns of thought escape this difficulty by assigning importance to a variety of factors and to the diversity of commitments undertaken by human beings. This multiplicity of factors, however, does not prevent pluralistic and process thinkers from using the historical method to create general visions of the human condition. It merely makes the quest for common themes more challenging and the resulting product more complex.

Demographic Method

Closely related to the historical method is the demographic method. While the historical method is qualitative in the sense that it issues in ideal types expressed in words, the demographic method is quantitative because it uses statistical data. The demographic method is the analysis of statistical data originally collected by government and other agencies for purposes other than scientific research. These numbers include crime statistics, voting results, tallies of membership in religious and other organizations, and vital statistics (births, deaths, and so on). This means that those who use the demographic method do not create their own information.

Demographic sociology, which began with the works of the Belgian Quételet in the nineteenth century, uses statistics to compare and contrast social groups. Durkheim, for example, used this method to show that the incidence of suicide was higher among people with few stable social ties than among those with many social ties.[18] This example shows the strength and the weakness of the demographic method. Its strength is that, as long as the statistics are somewhat accurate, this method can quickly dispel sweeping and misinformed generalizations about social groups and add support to some visions of the human condition rather than others. Thus, Durkheim's research cast doubt upon the idea that suicide was strictly a matter of "mental illness." The weakness of the demographic method follows from its strength. While it can detect trends and tendencies, it must remain mute about particular individuals and their projects. One cannot leap from statistical tallies to statements about what factors "cause" people to act in certain ways. The absurdity of such leaps is shown by the fact that they can be made in contradictory directions. Given the statistic that crime rates are higher in predominantly black neighborhoods than in predominantly white neighborhoods, some people draw the conclusion that blacks are inherently "prone to violence" while others draw the conclusion that "poverty and discrimination are the true causes of crime."[19] Neither of these interpretive leaps is warranted merely by the statistics. They must be judged in terms of wider visions of the human condition in which the statistics are merely one piece of evidence.

Uses The historical and the demographic methods are the basic procedures for carrying out social research without creating data. Their most important feature is that they can be used immediately by any human being who can read and count. If the aim of this book is to encourage people to embark on an adventure in self-understanding and to be responsible for their images of the human condition, a key step in realizing this aim is to encourage people to use the historical and demographic methods themselves. Perhaps the best way to begin to use these methods is for the individual to take a look at his stock of ideal types and to see whether or not they stand up to inspection. This is simply another way of saying that the first phase of self-understanding is clarification.

Participant Methods

In the historical and demographic methods, the human scientist weaves information gathered by others into a pattern of which the others might not have been aware. He is generally not present at the events that were the source of this information. In participant observation, on the other hand, the researcher is present at ongoing social activities. For example, if a sociologist is interested in studying the characteristics of work and social relations on an assembly line, he might become an assembly-line worker for a time and gain firsthand knowledge of the situation. For a study of mental hospitals he might take a job as an attendant in a mental hospital.[20] For an investigation of the lower-class black man's way of life, he might hang out with such people at their haunts.[21] Thus, the participant-observation method involves the researcher more in the creation of information than do the historical or the demographic methods.

The general problem of the participant method is that, while the activities witnessed by the sociologist are generally not undertaken at his direction, there is a question of how much influence his presence exerts on the content of activity. There is no way of knowing what the precise nature of the activity would be with the researcher absent. This problem has led to several attempts at solution. Most of them involve the use of secrecy and sometimes of outright deceit. The simplest measure is for the sociologist merely not to disclose his purposes to the group being studied. For example, if he is working on an assembly line he does not tell his fellow workers that he is a sociologist, and pretends to be just one of the boys. More complicated measures involve the use of hidden tape recorders and cameras to transcribe "spontaneous" activities.[22]

These tricks have been devised to get around the problem that human beings are capable of altering their activities upon receipt of new information. They are of very dubious ethical standing because they only succeed by keeping the people being studied in ignorance of their actual situation. They may also be ineffective for two reasons. First, there is no way of insuring that nobody will suspect the fraud. This factor becomes increasingly important as more people learn about the "techniques" of social research. Second, with respect to the use of hidden recording instruments, the ultimate purpose of direct observation is to learn the meanings behind human actions rather than to impose meanings on these actions. By simply viewing a given social interaction, one may not correctly interpret the meanings given by the participants. For example, seeing a man giving a boy some money will not reveal whether he is giving charity, giving his son an allowance or placing a bet.

Participant observation was first perfected by anthropologists who were interested in understanding systems of action and the meanings of these actions in groups with unfamiliar cultures (including different languages from those known by the anthropologists).[23] Here there could be no question of outright deceit because the anthropologist was obviously different from those he was studying and had to win their confidence before he could attain his research goals. Obviously, an Englishman or a Frenchman could not pass as the member of a tribe in the Amazonian rain forests or the Kalahari Desert. The ultimate aim of field work (the anthropologist's term for participant observation) is not so much for the researcher to share directly in the experiences felt by those he is studying as to capture their existence as a whole through their own frames of reference. Thus, the goal of the anthropologist is essentially to clarify the image of the human condition held by those he is studying. It is, of course, often the case that the people he is observing are not aware of these frames of reference, just as many of those reading this book are not fully aware of their visions of the human condition.

An important consideration in using the participant-observation method is that the investigator give an accurate report of what he has observed, rather than a commentary colored by his original views, biases, and orientations. This means that good participant observation involves the method of self-understanding in all its phases. It involves clarification because, without knowledge of one's image of the human condition, it is impossible to pick out one's biases. Generalization enters when the anthropologist is able to identify himself as a member of a particular culture, and relativization follows with the recognition that the culture he represents is one among many. Finally, commitment comes when the anthropologist dedicates himself to understanding the meanings of activities for others and describing the general patterns of these meanings as they cut across different groups. The fact that good participant observation involves the process of self-understanding as both its precondition and goal means that everyone who is along the road to self-understanding has automatically become a human scientist. Thus, such a person will be studying each group to which he belongs at the very time he is acting within that group. If he is fully committed to inquiry he will make the results of his investigations known to his colleagues and thereby increase the awareness necessary for intensifying freedom. In this case, human science becomes collective self-criticism.

The result of participant observation is a description of a way of life. No other method results in an answer to the broad question, What is it like to be a member of this group? The researcher may find the life-style he is observing to be preferable to his own. There are stories of anthropologists failing to come back from their field trips because they became so involved with the groups they were studying. This can be viewed as either a hazard or a benefit of using the method. Short of conversion to a new way of life, the method enables a person to explore the possibilities of a life different from the one he is leading, either through undertaking research himself or reading the reports of research done by others. One can get an idea of what different jobs are like, or what it would be like to live under different family arrangements. Since the participant-observation method embodies the process of self-understanding, it is disturbing to realize that the majority of studies in sociology that utilize the method are concerned with either downtrodden or deviant groups.[24] Delinquents, the unemployed, drug users, and mental patients represent only a narrow spectrum of the possibilities for human beings. It is also important to note that, although what is commonly called participant observation involves physical presence in a group, many of the same results can be gained through *imaginative* participation in groups. Novels, utopian literature, and histories are all arenas for the observation of groups and the exploration of new possibilities. It is in such imaginative participation that the historical and participant methods fuse.

NONPARTICIPANT OBSERVATION

It is not necessary to become a member of a group to study it firsthand. Nonparticipant observation is the method in which the researcher is on the scene of group activity, but holds himself apart from that activity to study certain aspects of human relations. This method is not as easy for the ordinary person to apply as participant observation, because most groups will not invite a researcher to study their activity unless they expect to gain something from the research. Thus, much nonparticipant observation has been carried out in bureaucratic organizations where managerial groups have allowed sociologists to study human relations in work settings, perhaps with the idea that the resulting research will reveal the sources of inefficiency and the ways of reducing it.[25] Since the nonparticipant observer does not become a member of the group he is studying and often attempts to remain as inconspicuous as possible (to avoid the "guinea pig effect"), his aim is usually not to grasp visions of the human condition, but to describe patterns of social relations. For example, in studying a group of office workers, the nonparticipant observer may note when official rules are broken, for what purpose and by whom. He may uncover networks of "informal organization" through which tasks get carried out when the official rules hinder efficiency. Alternatively, he may uncover patterns through which work is avoided or sabotage is performed. Participant observers, of course, are also capable of focusing on patterns of human relations (for example, hidden power structures, friendship cliques). If the nonparticipant observer remains unobtrusive enough, he has the advantage of not disturbing the pattern of relations in the group by adding a new member to it.

For the ordinary person, nonparticipant observation can best be done in public places. One may study the relations among waitresses in a restaurant, the behavior of political demonstrators, the avoidance patterns of pedestrians on a busy street or the relations among mechanics at a garage when one's car is being repaired. Questions that one might ask would be: Who seems to ask for advice and who gives it? If conflicts appear, what are they about? Do the official authority relations seem to hold, or are they breached? How much of their time do people spend working and how much "socializing"? One might want to compare relations at different restaurants, different service stations, different demonstrations, or among different families at a public beach or park. Nonparticipant observation can be a broadening experience which opens up new sensitivity to the range of social relations. All bus terminals are not the same; each discount department store has a slightly different work setting, leading to more or less harmony, efficiency, and individual initiative. Making nonparticipant observation a part of one's existence not only reduces boredom, but also gives one knowledge of the complexity of what at first sight seem to be the simplest of human relations.

SURVEY METHOD

The survey method involves the sociologist in creating his information far more than do the methods previously discussed. This method, which basically involves asking people questions and recording the responses, takes several different forms. When a researcher records the reply, either in writing or with the use of a tape recorder, the method is technically known as interviewing. When the respondent writes his answer out it is known as the questionnaire method. In either case, the questions may range from those requiring a brief reply indicating such facts as one's age, marital status, or father's occupation, to those demanding a more extended response indicating such things as the reasons why one went to college or what one thinks of social equality for racial minorities. A further distinction within this method involves whether the question is open ended or forced choice. Open-ended responses allow the respondent to improvise his own answers to the questions in his own words. Forced choices require the respondent to select an answer from a fixed set of alternatives. Which particular type of survey method is used depends, of course, upon the problem guiding inquiry. For example, if one is interested in political-party affiliation, the forced-choice questionnaire with brief reply might be most appropriate.

The survey method is currently the one most frequently used in sociology (perhaps because of its apparent simplicity) and also the most misused method. The most important pitfalls are those that follow from the failure to clarify divergent frames of reference. Asking questions is a normal human activity. However, most inquiries take place between people who share common frames of reference, use language in similar ways and, in general, are quite sensitive to the specific intentions of the question. This is by no means necessarily the case when hundreds or even thousands of people are asked to respond on a questionnaire or to an interviewer. Many of the people questioned may have little in common with the background, style of language, and interests of the researcher.[26] Thus, they may give different meanings to the questions than the researcher intended. This means that the respondents frequently misinterpret the questions and that the researcher often misinterprets the answers, leading to a situation in which the "new knowledge" is of low quality. A second difficulty is that questions are sometimes phrased in such a manner as to bias the response. This is the social science equivalent of the "loaded question" which appears in propaganda and in everyday life. For example, someone interested in attitudes regarding future space exploration might betray his bias by asking, "Do you think that we should waste any more money on space flight?" In an attempt to avoid such bias researchers try to devise neutral questions. Propagandists and advertisers, on the other hand, try to devise loaded questions ("You do like our product, don't you?"). Then they can report that 95 percent of those questioned prefer their product.

Another danger in survey research is generalizing from an inadequate base of information. For example, it would probably be a mistake to question the people in your sociology class about their reading habits and then conclude from the findings that Americans in general read the same amounts of the same things; college students are of course unlikely to be representative of the rest of the population. The people in your sociology class, however, might be representative of college students in general on this matter and, thus, generalizing the findings to all college students might not be a mistake. Propagandists make it a practice to generalize from an inadequate base of information. For example, they will use striking cases of demonstrations turning into riots to argue that all demonstrations tend toward riots. For sociologists, however, whether one assumes that the sample surveyed is representative of some wider group, such as Americans, the middle class, or even "people," should depend upon knowledge of both the sample and the larger group.

While, like all other methods, the survey method can be misused, it enables one to gain significant information when wisely applied. It is particularly helpful in the processes of generalization and relativization, because it enables one to identify those with whom one agrees and disagrees. In reading the results of surveys, people are sometimes amazed and sometimes relieved to find that there are many who agree with them on certain issues. This recognition may stop a person from thinking that he is mentally ill or deviant ("If I am the only one in the world who thinks this I must be crazy, but if many other people agree with me maybe there is some truth in what I think"). Further, when people find that they are in agreement in criticizing the present order, this recognition may give rise to joint action for social change. Surveys also provide information about where support for and opposition to social movements can be expected.[27] Thus, surveys help make the private problems of individuals into public issues.

The current drawbacks of survey research do not arise from the method itself, but from the way it has been used. In general, survey research has failed to ask crucial questions, and has often allowed for only those answers the researcher considered to be possible.[28] The processes of clarification and relativization of beliefs are both enhanced when new answers are given to old questions. Respondents can also benefit directly from the research when they are asked questions they had never before confronted and when they are presented with alternatives they had never before envisioned. This kind of inventive use of survey research creates a new social reality.

Depth Interviewing

While the ordinary person is primarily hindered from undertaking survey research by the lack of funds and facilities (for example, a computer), depth interviewing is even more difficult for the nonprofessional to carry out. In depth interviewing, subjects are asked to speak about their ideas and experiences with regard to basic values such as social equality, civil liberties, marital and parental relations, ethnic identification, and religious commitments. The interviewer takes notes or tapes the conversation, sometimes letting the respondent determine the direction of the discussion (nondirective interviewing) and sometimes attempting to guide the discussion through pointed questions (directive interviewing). The aim of the researcher is to find underlying themes in the responses of the subject which reveal tensions and ambivalence about one's role in the social structure, conflicting values, and fundamental vision of the human condition. For example, one might conduct depth interviews with working-class whites to determine the extent to which they are willing to apply the value of social equality in their personal relations. Do they carry racial prejudices against blacks? Are they willing to let any prejudices they have influence their attitudes and activities with respect to equal employment opportunities, open housing and the integration of schools? If they are prejudiced and willing to discriminate, how do they justify their attitudes and actions? It is clear that many people would not submit to a depth interview unless they trusted the researcher personally or trusted his professional integrity.

Depth interviews differ from survey research and are similar to participant observation, because they allow for the analysis of visions of the human condition rather than particular attitudes. Thus, the best depth interviewers are those who have carried through the processes of generalization and relativization, enabling them to be conscious of their own world-view and sensitive to the world-view of the subject. Depth interviewing combines the difficulties of survey research and nonparticipant observation. Like survey research, it may involve asking questions about which the person has never thought deeply; and like nonparticipant observation, it may produce a "guinea pig" effect. Further, it is difficult to derive generalizations from depth interviewing, because the sample is usually small and the interviewer must be sophisticated enough not to impose his own agenda on the conversation. Like participant observation, depth interviewing demands that the researcher keep his own biases in abeyance.

In depth interviewing, the researcher is often concerned with identifying images of which the subject is not fully conscious. The subject may believe that he is committed to social equality, but his responses may show that in many cases he is actually committed to white supremacy. The aim of uncovering "covert culture" involves certain ethical dilemmas. To reach his goal, the researcher must conceal it from the subject in order to avoid defensive tactics and pat answers. Thus, the researcher must ask for trust at the same time he refuses to give it. This tactic involves a certain degree of manipulation.

If one is willing to forget the ethical dilemmas, approximations to depth interviewing can be made in ordinary life. On buses and trains, and at vacation resorts, people removed from their everyday social relations are often willing to speak freely about themselves, their problems, and their attitudes about social relations. They seek opportunities to converse in order to test their ideas against a neutral judge and because they feel more secure away from their normal social contacts. Also, in expressing themselves freely to a stranger they do not risk the tangible punishments they might suffer from expressing themselves freely at work, among friends or even in the family. It is possible to turn such conversations with strangers into depth interviews by guiding them toward the discussion of particular attitudes about society, and then looking for inconsistencies, tensions, and hidden motivations.

There is much to be learned about images of the human condition from such conversations, particularly if one makes sure to find out the social background data about the stranger (type of work, degree of education, religious affiliation, ethnicity, geographical residence, and family background). Then it may be possible to trace back some of the attitudes expressed to social factors, allowing one to reconstruct the stranger's image of the human condition. Whether or not one undertakes such a project will depend upon whether he is willing to manipulate people in this way.

Experimental Small Groups

The method of experimental small groups involves the sociologist the most deeply in creating his own information. In general, small-group research brings together people who would not otherwise form a group (and who may never have even seen one another before), and provides a situation in which these people interact. The basic assumption behind this method is that the behavior observed under the conditions contrived by the researcher is not significantly different from what would happen under similar conditions in everyday social life. For example, the behaviors observed in a contest set up by the researcher may be used as a model of what goes on in business competition.

The problems investigated through the experimental small-groups method have varied from trying to determine how a group can influence an individual's attitudes or beliefs, to attempting to find out how much pain one person will administer to another.[29] Many studies utilizing small groups are of particular interest to large organizations, especially business and military conglomerates. These organizations are interested in the question, How can workers (or soldiers) become more efficient? Some sociologists attempt to answer this question by having experimental small groups perform tasks under varying conditions.[30] They see how performance varies as conditions change (different lighting, presence or absence of music, varying styles of leadership).[31] Sociologists undertake these studies, not because they want to exploit the worker, but because they are being funded by the managements of the organizations. It would be interesting to find out what questions would be studied if researchers had a free hand in selecting their problems. It is also interesting to note that labor unions have not yet seen fit to support counter-research on such questions as, How can management be made to produce more humane working conditions?

The experimental small-group method has also been used in trying to understand international relations and relations between businesses (What are the causes and cures of conflict?). In such "simulations of the real world" individuals are made to represent such units as nations or corporations and then to play a game that supposedly parallels what happens in actual conflicts.[32] This procedure rests on the questionable assumption that organizations are "things" that act like human beings. Further, and even more important, despite the use of the game metaphor in politics ("Nixon's game plan") and business ("the money game"), games do not share many significant features with other aspects of human existence. In a game, it is assumed that the participants know the rules, the rules do not change in the midst of the contest, all are aiming at the same goal (victory), the rules declare a winner and an end to the game, and one person's loss is another person's gain. None of these conditions seems to hold in most life situations. Further, most games do not involve life-or-death decisions.

Much of the research utilizing small groups can be criticized from the standpoint that most experimental situations do not reflect life situations in important respects. Who cares to generalize from one contrived situation to another? Attempts have been made to take account of this criticism by utilizing natural groups, that is, groups that are already in existence, such as work groups, school classes and the like. The validity of the results of these studies depends to a large extent upon how real the participants viewed the situation.

The small-group method need not involve any separation between researchers and participants. In its widest sense the method includes investigations where the roles of researcher and participant are one. Utopian communities such as the Oneida experiment and Brook Farm, as well as some hippie communes and radical collectives, can be understood as experiments in seeing what life would be like if certain principles and rules were put into effect. Small-group studies of a more private nature frequently are undertaken, as when a married couple attempt to live together with full equality and dignity for each. In the case of such living experiments, the method of experimental small groups becomes one with the method of participant observation and the wider process of self-understanding. Every group situation can be viewed as an experiment in human existence, and can be judged and criticized by those participating. It is, of course, to the advantage of elite groups to make people believe that group situations fulfilling elite purposes are not experiments but are eternal parts of the human condition.

Figure 4.1. THE CLASSIFICATION OF METHODS

Least Creation of Data by Sociologist	Most Creation of Data by Sociologist

Historical Method
    Demographic Method
        Participant Observation
            Nonparticipant Observation
                Survey Method
                    Depth-Interview Method
                        Experimental Small-Group Method

METHOD IN REVIEW

Sociological methods range from those in which the researcher analyzes and reshapes information gathered by others, to those in which he creates his own information. The basic sociological method is the historical and demographic method which uses available documents to construct images of the human condition (ideal types). These ideal types form the context in which more specific sociological methods are used. Participant methods involve the presence of the sociologist in group situations, attempting to grasp the meanings behind the behaviors of group members. Surveys require the sociologist to create his information by asking people questions and having them respond either vocally or in writing. Finally, the method of experimental small groups requires the sociologist to bring together people and contrive a situation in which they must act with respect to one another. While in its most narrow definition, this method involves the sociologist most deeply in creating his own information, in its widest sense every small group can be conceived as an experiment in human existence. This is because human beings are continually contriving the conditions of their existence, with or without the help of social scientists. Where the small-group method meets the historical and participant methods is where the sociologist makes people aware of their own experiments.

Despite the fact that the preceding overview of major sociological methods was brief, the diversity of methods is readily apparent. No one method is inherently better than another. Rather, a method is more or less appropriate to answer a given question. Certain prediction of future events is not possible using any of these methods, but it is human freedom rather than faulty method that is responsible for this situation. Certain prediction is valuable for engineers who want to manipulate things. Do we really want a class of human engineers who manipulate people for the ends of those who pay them? Fortunately, it is not even necessary to answer this question because sociological methods achieve an understanding of the present and of various possibilities for the future. Through the use of these methods one can choose with fuller awareness to commit oneself to a specific future and help to create it. The best way to block the emergence of a class of human engineers is to become a sociologist yourself.

THE HISTORICAL METHOD IN USE

Lipset, S. M.; Trow, M.; and Coleman, J.S. *Union Democracy*. Glencoe, Ill.: Free Press, 1956.

The historical method is best adapted to describing the general organizational patterns and processes through which human beings act on their projects. Any image of the human condition developed through the historical method draws some conclusions about the projects most likely to be successful in a given social structure. Those who dispute such conclusions have the alternatives of generating an entirely new image or of revising the existing image. The process of revision may be carried out through a "critical case study." In the critical case study, an organization is selected that does not display the characteristics defined in the existing image and then an attempt is made to explain the divergence from expectation.

An example of a critical case study is the analysis of the International Typographical Union conducted by Seymour Lipset and his associates. Lipset disputed the contention of Robert Michels that democratic decision making is impossible in large formal organizations. Selecting the International Typographical Union as an organization that had a two-party democracy rather than a single ruling elite, Lipset attempted to explain why this organization was not an oligarchy by seeing how its membership and social structure differed from the pattern within less democratic unions. He showed, among other things, that members of the ITU formed closer communities than other unionized workers because they worked in relatively small shops and often at odd hours. They also had a tradition of strong local organization and decentralized bargaining patterns with employers. Such factors encouraged concern with union affairs by members, the appearance of multiple power centers within the union, and built-in checks upon the seizure of power by small cliques. Added to these factors were the relatively high incomes, educational attainments and political sophistication of members. Thus, Lipset was able successfully to challenge and *revise* Michels' thesis that oligarchy is inevitable in large formal organizations. He did not argue against the claim that there is a *tendency* toward oligarchy in such organizations, but maintained that this tendency can be mitigated by particular constellations of social, cultural, and personal factors.

The kind of critical case study done by Lipset can be applied to challenge many sweeping claims about the nature of social organization. For example, some people claim that democracy is impossible outside a capitalist economic system. In order to challenge this thesis one might look for a nation in which democracy functioned in a socialist or semi-socialist economy, and attempt to see how the danger of using the economy as a political weapon was avoided. Or, one might challenge the thesis that grades are necessary to motivate learning by seeking out examples of successful experiments in ungraded courses and seeing how motivation was sustained.

THE DEMOGRAPHIC METHOD IN USE

Durkheim, Emile. *Suicide.* Glencoe, Ill.: Free Press, 1951.

Perhaps the most famous example of the demographic method in sociology is Emile Durkheim's study of suicide rates. Durkheim's major concern was to refute the claims that suicide was the result of variations in climate, hereditary factors, individual psychological disturbances or sheer imitation and crowd contagion, and to advance the thesis that rates of suicide are related to the degree to which human beings are integrated into social groups. Using publicly available statistics on suicide rates, Durkheim showed that explanations of suicide that did not take social integration into account could not be supported by the evidence. For example, some writers maintained that temperature had a direct effect on the number of suicides, but Durkheim showed that rate of suicide did not vary directly with temperature change.

In supporting his own claim that suicide is a function of the absence of social bonds, Durkheim linked suicide rates with three variables: religion, family, and political situation. He found that suicide rates were higher among Protestants than Catholics (Protestantism has an individualistic theology and Catholicism a more communal theology), among unmarried than married people, among childless married couples than married couples with children, and in times of political crisis and nationalist agitation than in times of political tranquility.

These conclusions helped support and advance Durkheim's central idea that social structure functions somewhat independently of individual personality characteristics in determining human activity.

Similar studies to Durkheim's can be done using publicly available statistics. For example, incidence of various kinds of crime, of automobile accidents, of divorces or of civil violence can be correlated with social structural factors to determine how far it is possible to explain these phenomena on the bases of personality, organic or environmental factors. Does the "long, hot summer" theory of civil violence make sense? What about the hereditary theory of crime? Such topics are continually studied by sociologists and you can begin to do research on them now if you are interested in any of them.

The Participant Method in Use

Goffman, Erving. *Asylums.* Garden City, N.Y.: Doubleday, 1961.

While the participant method can be used in any social group to which the investigator can gain access, some of its most striking applications have been carried out in organizations closed off from the general public. An example of a significant and socially critical use of the participant method is Erving Goffman's study of the life and worldview of inmates in a large mental hospital. Guided by the assumption that "a good way to learn about (the world of the mental patient) is to submit oneself in the company of the members to the daily round of petty contingencies to which they are subject," Goffman took the role of assistant to the athletic director of the hospital and then "passed the day with patients, avoiding sociable contact with the staff and the carrying of a key." The top management of the hospital knew of his aims in advance, so he did not have to worry that his research would be cut off precipitously.

In penetrating the "world" of the inmate, Goffman found that mental patients attempt to maintain as much personal integrity as possible by appropriating property and space for their own uses and trying to keep up an appearance of dignity in a debasing situation. He also discovered that the official ideology of the hospital—that patients should cooperate with the staff in effecting a cure—was not shared by the inmates. Instead, the inmates showed "a self-justifying definition of their own situation and a prejudiced view of non-members, in this case, doctors, nurses, attendants, and relatives."

Goffman's research shows some of the strengths as well as some of the problems of the participant method. He was able to learn things about the "world" of the mental patient that could probably not be discovered through the historical, demographic, survey or experimental methods. However, he admits that his results were "partisan" (biased in favor of the values of the mental patients) and not amenable to verification by quantitative methodologies (statistical measurement would have been difficult for a participant observer). These difficulties, of course, are only significant if one believes that sociology can be "value-free" and should employ a natural-science model. More important, perhaps, is the ethical problem. Goffman was able to gather his information because people thought he was an assistant to the athletic director (when "pressed," he avowed to being "a student of recreation and community life"). He probably could not have been as effective an observer if he had announced his intentions in advance. This ethical problem of concealing intention haunts most participant research, and the choice is between gaining the insights and critiques produced by people like Goffman and making sociological research more honest.

The Nonparticipant Method in Use

Blau, Peter M. *The Dynamics of Bureaucracy.* Chicago: University of Chicago Press, 1963.

Like the participant method, nonparticipant observation is useful in revealing patterns of social interaction that would be difficult to discover with more indirect methods. An example of nonparticipant observation is Peter M. Blau's study of a division of a state employment agency. Blau began with the idea that organizations do not always function according to the principles set down in the rule book. His observations confirmed in many different instances the existence of informal networks of relations that violated the spirit, if not the letter, of the official code. For example, employment interviewers were supposed to complete detailed forms on job requests for workers, provide counseling to those seeking employment and find the most qualified worker for a given job. However, the situation in which the interviewers actually found themselves did not lend itself to the fulfillment of these norms. Since requests for workers came sporadically and in large chunks, and since these requests were usually for relatively unskilled labor, there did not seem to be good reasons to spend time filling out detailed forms, deciding who was most capable of filling a position or counseling potential employees. Further, performance of the agency was judged according to how many people were placed, not according to the professional quality of counseling or to the level of accuracy in fitting individuals to specific positions. Thus, instead of living up to the spirit of the rules, interviewers placed people on a first-come, first-served basis.

From these observations, Blau drew the conclusion that informal relations functioning outside or even against the rules often fulfill formal organizational goals more efficiently. The state employment interviewers he observed were actually working to attain organizational purposes by more effective means than those prescribed in the rule book. Of course, behind this situation was a kind of organizational hypocrisy. While officially interviewers were supposed to be judged on the quality of their work, in actuality they were judged only on the quantity of placements. Such hypocrisy is probably responsible for a great deal of the kinds of informal organization Blau discovered. Workers grasp that what the rules prescribe is not what is really expected of them. This hypothesis, of course, can be tested by readers of this book as they observe formal organizations.

The Survey Method in Use

Stouffer, Samuel. *Communism, Conformity, and Civil Liberties.* Garden City, N.Y.: Doubleday, 1955.

One of the most important uses of the survey method is to determine how different groups in a society are aligned on given issues. By eliciting attitudes on various issues of public concern, the researcher can gather information on which groups are likely to favor and oppose certain policies. Further, attitude research can affirm or question generalizations about the perspectives of different groups. An example of this use of the survey method is Samuel Stouffer's study of attitudes toward the protection of civil liberties in the United States during the early 1950s—a time at which Senator Joseph McCarthy was attempting to mobilize public sentiment against the American left wing. Stouffer's study was based on two independently chosen random samples of the American people (a "national cross section") and two samples of community leaders (mayors and American Legion commanders). Stouffer was interested in determining which groups in the American population were most favorably disposed towards limiting such civil liberties as freedom of speech and association to diminish an internal communist threat. In order to reach his goal, Stouffer asked such questions as: "If a person wanted to make a speech in your community against churches and religions, should he be allowed to speak or not?" He found generally that the community leaders were more likely to express attitudes of tolerance to nonconformity than was the population in general. For example, while more than 60 percent of the community leaders claimed that a person should be allowed to make a speech against religions, 60 percent of the national cross section would not allow such a speech.

Stouffer's work has been used to support the theory of "democratic elitism" which holds that the protection of individual rights and democratic processes is best assured by the upper middle class and is somewhat endangered by the lower middle and working classes. This interpretation has been challenged by the claim that, even according to Stouffer's data, tolerance varies directly according to educational attainment, not directly according to class, and that most civil liberties issues are not of great importance to many lower-middle and working-class people. The use of surveys to support and undermine images of the human condition shows that they cannot stand alone as examples of "pure research" but that, instead, they have ramifications for the adequacy and fruitfulness of programs for social stability and change.

The Depth Interview Method in Use

Becker, Howard, et al. *The Boys in White.* Chicago: University of Chicago Press, 1961.

The depth interview is best adapted to probing ambivalence in attitudes and to uncovering sentiments that lie below the surface of socially accepted opinions and ideologies. An example of research using the depth interview method is Howard Becker's study of value conflict in medical students. While Becker was primarily conducting a participant observation study of the attitudes of medical students toward the medical profession, he spoke to individual students at length in conversations that approximated depth interviews. Becker notes that sociologists normally attempt to get "beneath" the idealistic ideologies of people and penetrate to their "latent" concrete interests. In his study of medical students Becker found himself confronting a reverse situation. He defines the subculture of medical students as one of "ritualized cynicism," in which a student who expresses any idealistic or altruistic sentiments will be ridiculed. Therefore, in his private conversations with students Becker attempted to pierce the conventional cynicism and bring out any idealistic motivations he could elicit. Rather than asking pointed questions that would reveal motives of self-interest, he encouraged expressions of idealism by speaking about topics in which they seemed to have "impractical" interests. He found that, despite the oppressive features of the role of medical student, many of the students maintained altruistic concerns that coexisted with their cynicism and concern for future security. This experience led Becker to the conclusion that sociologists should begin their research neither with the assumption that ulterior motives always underlie expressed motives nor with the assumption that people are as good as they say they are. Rather, they should begin with the hypothesis that people may have multiple motivations and that they may hold conflicting motives at different times.

Becker's use of the depth interview method raises some questions about its validity. How much does the interviewer have to intrude into the situation before the response he elicits is simply a function of his persistence? For example, how many of the medical students' altruistic responses were fabricated to please Becker? Further, how significant are suppressed motivations for actual social relations when the group structure imposes and enforces a conventional set of attitudes? Finally, is the hypothesis that people may be ambivalent any less dogmatic than the hypotheses that they mean what they say or that their expressed motives are screens behind which they hide their real motives? None of these questions renders the depth interview useless; they simply show the difficulties involved in understanding human motivations, attitudes, and sentiments.

The Experimental Group Method in Use

White, Ralph, and Lippitt, Ronald. *Autocracy and Democracy.* New York: Harper, 1960.

In the experimental group method the researcher creates groups and controls the environment so that he can determine whether certain consequences appear upon the introduction of given activities or relations. One of the more interesting series of small-group experiments was carried out by Lewin, Lippitt, and White on hobby and play groups of ten-year-old boys. While the designs of the various experiments are complex, the aim was to determine whether the quantity of work accomplished and the satisfaction of members with the group would be influenced by the style of the adult group leadership. Three types of groups were created according to three different styles of leadership—autocratic, democratic, and laissez faire (anarchic). Generally, the investigators found that in democratically organized groups the members showed the highest work motivation, the most originality in work projects and the greatest satisfaction with the group. Laissez faire organization, on the other hand, was characterized by lower productivity than democracy, poorer quality of work, and less satisfaction with the group. Finally, while autocratic organization resulted in the highest quantity of work done, originality was low, dependence was high, there was little satisfaction with the group, and, most important, there were high levels of discontent which were expressed by scapegoating, destruction of property, rebellion, dropping out of the group, and wild behavior when the autocratic leader was withdrawn.

The Lewin-Lippitt-White experiments demonstrate the manipulative character of small-group research, as well as its cultural boundedness. Is it ethical to impose autocratic leadership on a group of children who cannot understand why they are being subjected to this sytem? How much were the results of this research influenced by the fact that it was conducted in the United States, which has a democratic ideology, rather than in a society characterized by more authoritarian ideologies and institutions? While many small-group experiments show great ingenuity, use of the method raises moral questions and it is not easily applied, if it can be applied at all, in ordinary life.

5
HUMAN ACTION

The past four chapters have been devoted to describing the ways in which the human condition can be studied. They ranged from the most general consideration of how human beings can orient themselves to their situations as scientists to the more specific questions of the methods that they can use to analyze these situations. With this preceding discussion in mind, it is time to begin investigating the content of social existence. The presentation of the content of sociology will be, of course, from the viewpoint of process thought, and will stress the pattern of opportunities for human freedom present in the contemporary world, as well as the many obstacles to its attainment.

The content of sociology is the human condition, the basic components of that condition, and the relations among those components. Throughout the history of social thought, the major issues dividing competing perspectives have centered around different interpretations of the nature of these components and how they are linked together. In American sociology there are two general perspectives presently vying for dominance. Each is based on a view of which human experiences it is important for sociologists to investigate. One of these views is based on a restrictive interpretation of human experience, while the other is rooted in a more expansive understanding of experience. *Restrictive empiricism* has been the major current in American sociology up until recently, but now it is being challenged by a vigorous movement promoting *expansive empiricism*.

RESTRICTIVE EMPIRICISM

The root idea of all empiricism is that whatever can be known by human beings appears in their experience.[1] Therefore, according to empiricists, what is believed in but is not experienced (for example, many notions of God) is not an object of knowledge, but is an object of faith. Since factual accuracy is near the core of all science, scientific investigation is based on an empirical interpretation of knowledge.

Restrictive empiricism holds that only certain human experiences are open to scientific investigation. These experiences fall within the range of what is thought to be "publicly observable" or capable of being known independently by any human being with the full use of his senses.[2] Thus, restrictive empiricists argue that inquiry into the human condition should be limited to that area of experience that can be known through the five senses—sight, sound, taste, smell, and touch. This means that restrictive empiricists study human *behavior,* or that part of the process of human action which can be "externally observed."

Restrictive empiricism became popular in sociology mainly because many social scientists thought that it was the foundation of the natural sciences. They reasoned that, if natural science restricted itself to studying what could be observed through the senses, then social science could only be successful if it placed the same limitations upon itself. This decision to follow the lead of natural science led to the development of many of the methods discussed in the preceding chapter, particularly the demographic, survey and experimental-small-group techniques. Social scientists believe that by using these techniques they could avoid the difficulties involved in trying to find out what was going on "inside people's heads." Governmental statistics on suicide rates were seen as objective, in the sense that they referred to events that could be observed through the senses. The web of feeling in which the suicide was enmeshed could be factored out of the scientific description and left to the novelist or playwright. Responses to a questionnaire on political-party preferences were also held to be observable, at least by anyone who understood the language in which the responses were written. For many purposes, the meaning of this preference to the respondent could be ignored. This was particularly true if the aim of the social scientist was to predict the general trends in voting behavior. The results of experiments aimed at finding the factors influencing the output of work groups were considered objective. Meanwhile, the fundamental principles of economic activity operating within the contemporary human condition, such as organizational growth, could be held constant and put out of awareness. Finally, with feelings, meanings, and principles left out of social research, many social scientists concluded that their task was to find out the factors that determined human behavior rather than the structural limitations on the development of human freedom. This lack of attention to freedom was a direct result of adopting restrictive empiricism and trying to imitate the natural sciences.

Restrictive empiricism has, we believe, a built-in failing which has led to the development of opposing interpretations of experience. This weakness can be grasped by considering the claim that the responses to a questionnaire are scientific data because they are observable through the senses. It is apparent that the least significant feature of the responses is that they are publicly observable. The questions themselves are put in a language that must be understood by the respondent if his answers are to be useful. This understanding, essential to the purpose of the questionnaire, is not publicly observable. Further, the very purpose of the questionnaire is to gain knowledge of some aspect of the human condition. This purpose is not publicly observable, but is intended by the scientist. Finally, the observable responses to the questionnaire are merely symbols of the meanings that respondents have expressed. Thus, a complex network of understandings, intentions, and meanings is necessary to make sense of the questionnaire as a tool of research. From this viewpoint, the questionnaire is merely the tip of a vast iceberg. It is, of course, possible to ignore the rest of the iceberg and study only the tip. However, in choosing to do this, the scientist should realize that he is taking for granted large chunks of human experience in the absence of which his research would not be possible. This means that the results of his research will be indicators of underlying processes which he has cut himself off from studying. It also means that his thought about the human condition will be inadequate to account for his own activity as a scientist. Like all other human activities, scientific inquiry is enmeshed in a set of feelings, goals, principles, and choices which can only be understood by opening inquiry to the entire field of experience.[3]

EXPANSIVE EMPIRICISM

The weaknesses of restrictive empiricism were already apparent to some thinkers in the nineteenth century, but have only come to the attention of a large number of sociologists in recent years.[4] One response to these weaknesses is to appeal to principles outside of human experience, such as a deity or an absolute spirit that cannot be observed, but that are supposedly responsible for making sense of the "inner life." Similarly, appeal can be made to abstract entities such as the Self or Society, which do not appear directly in human experience except as words. From this perspective, some entity called the Self, or some object called Society, stands behind human experience and causes particular experiences to occur. For example, some people claim that "bad individuals" are the cause of crime, while others retort that the real roots of crime are found in "society." Anybody who has engaged in such debates can testify how arid they become and how they seem to dissolve into confusion. This aridity and confusion are the result of discussing human activity in terms of entities that are not experienced as "things." Neither the self nor society are things that cause other things to happen. They are processes into which particular human activities such as producing, consuming, learning, and deciding are knit, and are, therefore, much more like results than like causes.[5] What view of experience can one adopt in order to be aware both of the weaknesses of restrictive empiricism and unwilling to appeal to entities beyond experience? The answer to this question is really present in the preceding discussion. The scientific alternative to restrictive empiricism is an expansive empiricism which takes account of the full range of human experiences, including feeling, meaning, principle, and freedom. It attempts to link these experiences to one another and to the "tip of the iceberg"—publicly observable behavior. Thus, it is not a way of throwing out the vast amount of social science research that has been done in the twentieth century with the tools of demographic analysis, survey research, and experimental small groups. Instead, it is a way of trying to make sense out of this research and relating it to more fundamental human concerns. One way of understanding expansive empiricism is as an attempt to integrate the historical and participant methods with the other methods. The historical method has been the major means through which the meanings and principles of human activity have been revealed, while participant methods have been the means through which the feelings and choices in human activity have been disclosed. Thus, the historical and participant methods help to "make sense" out of the results of the demographic, survey and experimental-small-group methods.

Expansive empiricism is basic to a humanistic perspective on sociology and, therefore, to the process of self-understanding. In order to embark on the quest for self-understanding it is necessary to open oneself to the full range of human experience without any preconceptions about where it necessarily begins and ends.[6] Restrictive empiricists did not intend to place obstacles in the way of self-understanding, but they ended up doing so because their doctrine forced them to ignore significant phases of experience, or at least to slip these phases in through the back door and under the cover of "observable behavior." The case of restrictive empiricism shows how closely intertwined are the categories of human fact and human value. Through cutting off sociological inquiry at an arbitrary point, the restrictive empiricists also placed barriers in the way of attaining freedom. This is particularly ironic because the restrictive empiricists claimed that their "behavioral" human science would vastly increase the scope of human freedom by providing people with knowledge of the conditions under which particular kinds of events occur in social existence.[7]

Expansive empiricism has been developed by a number of philosophers and sociologists throughout the nineteenth and twentieth centuries, including such figures as William James, Henri Bergson, Edmund Husserl, Maurice Hauriou, and Georges Gurvitch. It has influenced American sociology through the works of Charles Horton Cooley, George Herbert Mead, Florian Znaniecki, Pitirim Sorokin, and Talcott Parsons. Its spirit has been strikingly described by Georges Gurvitch, who states that human experience breaks without cease its own frames of reference: "Like a true Proteus [experience] escapes us when we believe that we grasp it; we are made fools by it when we believe we have penetrated its secret, we are its victims when we believe we have freed ourselves from it, even if only for an instant."[8] The key to expansive empricism (called by James "radical empiricism" and by Gurvitch "hyper-empiricism") is that all human experience that can be described has a component of sense and feeling, is in process and is in some measure conceptually constructed. Thus, all experience has an element of immediacy (sense data and felt process) and mediacy (concepts and structured processes): "The effective experience that we oppose to arbitrary philosophical interpretations, such as lived experience, everyday experience or constructed experience, is always mediate to some degree. It is a point of intermediary spheres between the immediate and the constructed. . ."[9]

In order to understand fully the insight contained in expansive empiricism, it is necessary to perform a revolution in ordinary thinking. One helpful aid towards making this revolution is to imagine experience as a field—i.e., a somewhat amorphous moving mass rather than a specific and sharply defined object. You will notice that we did not say that you should imagine *your* experience as a field. For the expansive empiricist, the self appears *within* experience, rather than experience belonging to a self. This means that experience is the fundamental category and not the self. It is another way of stating the major point of the first chapter—that the self is process, not property.

Once you have grasped the image of a field, it is necessary to move on to the point that experience is a special kind of field. Experience is a field of happenings, expanding and contracting, sometimes moving quickly and sometimes more slowly, sometimes unified and sometimes diverse, sometimes smooth and sometimes jagged. Sometimes feeling predominates in the field, at other times relatively precise objects are dominant, at still other times the center of attention is relations among actions and actors, and at yet other times the very processes of change are at the forefront. Any complete description of a given experience will contain each of the major aspects of experience —sense and feeling, objects, relations, and processes. However, each given experience will tend to emphasize one of these aspects over the others. Thus, experience is always moving in the direction of one or another of its major aspects.

Each of the major aspects of experience can be given a name and made the basis of a type of experience. The more experience moves in the direction of sense and feeling, the more it can be called *lived experience*. Lived experience is the most primitive form of experience, and one may suppose that the closest human beings ever come to it in its pure form is when they are infants confronting a whirl of sense and feeling that has not yet been blocked out into objects. Sometimes people attempt to wrench themselves back into lived experience through taking hallucinogenic drugs (such as LSD or marijuana), or through encasing themselves in an environment of loud music, incense, and flashing lights. Whether or not such efforts are successful in liberating experience from well-defined objects, they show that a number of people in the contemporary world are looking for a foundation to their experience beyond the definitions that they have been taught.

The more experience moves in the direction of marked off objects, the more it can be called *cultural experience.* In cultural experience, parts of the field of experience are detached from the rest and made into more permanent features of existence. Unlike lived experience, which is a humming and buzzing confusion, cultural experience is relatively orderly and regularized. Most of the experiences of everyday life are cultural, in the sense that they are of objects that have names in an ordinary language and have usages that are known by those who identify them. Similarly, the experiences that scientists speak about in specialized languages are cultural, in the sense that those who understand the languages can identify them out of the total field of experience. For most people most of the time cultural experience is at the center of existence.

The more experience moves in the direction of ongoing relations between actions and actors, the more it can be called *social experience.* Social experience relates to such intergroup and interpersonal processes as competition, conflict, cooperation, exchange, and love. These relations are present wherever human activity appears and are not linked specifically to any set of cultural experiences. Nearly all human experience contains a social element, even those portions of experience which seem to be the most "private" and personal. Much personal experience is in the form of a conversation, a dialogue or an argument, in which the individual "talks to himself."[10] This internal conversation may embody such processes as conflict and cooperation between different tendencies towards action. Sometimes the conflict becomes so severe that it becomes difficult to speak of a single personality. Other personal experience, particularly creative activity, is undertaken with potential consumers, users, or appreciators in mind. In these experiences, the creator at least implies a possible future cooperative relation between his producing activity and the consuming activities of others.

Finally, the more experience moves in the direction of the processes of acting themselves, the more it can be called *creative experience.*

Creative experience makes sense out of the ways in which cultural experience arises from its lived and social matrix. As Gurvitch noted, human experience breaks without cease its own frames of reference. This aspect of novelty, freshness and dynamism is the creative component of experience. It is through creative processes, such as inventing and perfecting tools, creating new patterns of symbols, devising and appreciating products, and testing systems of rules for coordinating activity, that cultural experience becomes blocked off from lived experience. Thus, creative activity continually organizes and reorganizes the rest of experience. Since human existence takes place in time, and since time is irreversible, there are always new challenges, opportunities, and barriers appearing in human existence. In its purest form, creative experience comes close to the sheer intuition of change and process.[11] From there it shades off into the experiences of activity, effort, challenge and novelty.

Figure 5.1. THE TYPES OF HUMAN EXPERIENCE

	Subjective and Private	*Objective and Public*
Contents /	Lived Experience	Cultural Experience
Processes /	Creative Experience	Social Experience

DIRECTIONS OF HUMAN EXPERIENCE

Lived, cultural, social, and creative experience are the four directions in human experience. In the ever-shifting field of experience, one or another of these comes to the forefront and then fades away to make place for another. Viewing experience as a field makes it difficult to make hard and fast distinctions between the contents of experience and the processes of experiencing, or between subjects who experience and objects that are experienced. Of course, the four directions of experience are characterized by varying degrees of content and process, of subjectivity and objectivity. For example, lived experience has a primacy of content since its core is sensation and feeling. It is also relatively subjective because it is difficult to communicate and is closely related to specific states of the organism. Cultural experience also has a primacy of content since its core is the blocked-out and identifiable object. However, it is relatively objective, because it forms the basis of communication (language is an important phase of cultural experience) and is relatively independent of specific states of any particular organism. Social experience has a primacy of process, because it refers to interpersonal, interactional, and intergroup relations. These relations can be about any conceivable content. There can be cooperation in making weapons as well as in making medicines. Social experience is also relatively objective because it is generally centered around the interlinking of regularized activities, such as the competition between political parties, the conflict between warring states, the cooperation among members of an athletic team or the exchanges between buyers and sellers. Such relations are often quite independent of the particular organisms taking part in them. Finally, creative experience also has a primacy of process, because its core is the very flow of action. Like the relations making up social experience, the activity making up creative experience can work upon any conceivable content from a poem to a hammer. Creative experience, however, is relatively subjective because it tends to be highly individualized and, although its ultimate aim is usually a sharable cultural experience, it cannot be readily communicated before its completion. Thus, while there are no sharp lines that can be drawn between process and content, and subjectivity and objectivity, or between the four directions in experience, each direction has its distinguishing characteristics; these conceptual distinctions are rarely experienced separately.

The field of experience is always moving more in one direction than in the others. If you have been able to picture experience as a dynamic field, you will by now be able to grasp its ebbs and flows, and its changes in direction, as existence unfolds. Heightened awareness of the characteristics of experience is itself an immediate benefit of expansive empiricism. It is a benefit that cannot be provided by restrictive empiricism, because this view carves out certain phases of experience as being worthy of scientific attention and ignores the others. However, the importance of expansive empiricism goes far beyond its ability in aiding a person to make more immediate sense out of experience. It also provides a fundamental perspective for the study of human action.

EXERCISE

Try to experience your activities consciously as you go through the day. Which types of experience seem to predominate? When are you most immersed in cultural experience? lived experience? social experience? creative experience? What contexts seem to encourage each experience? What contexts discourage each type of experience?

HUMAN ACTION

Every science takes from the field of human experience a class of events, objects, processes or happenings that serve as its subject matter for analysis and description. The definition of this subject matter can be called the *scope* of the science. For example, restrictive empiricists have defined the scope of sociology as the class of "publicly" observable human behaviors, or even as the study of the "forms" of social relations (competition, domination, exchange, and so on), the investigation of groups, the study of rule-bound and purposive behaviors, and many other slices of experience.[12] There have frequently been heroic efforts to attempt to carve out a special niche for sociology that would distinguish it clearly from the other social sciences, such as political science, economics, anthropology, and jurisprudence. Thus, some have hoped that sociology would become the master social science, synthesizing all the results of the other social sciences into descriptions of the general patterns of historical development.[13] Others have advocated that sociology confine itself to investigating the linkages between different "areas" of human existence, such as the economy, the "political system," and the "culture."[14] Still others have observed that sociologists seem to study whatever the other social sciences have ignored in their investigations of the human condition.[15] According to this interpretation, since no other social science was taking an interest in such subjects as the family and race relations, sociology got to work on them. Related to this view is the idea that sociology arose as a result of the new problems created by the indirect consequences of industrialization and urbanization. Nobody specifically intended that industrialization and urbanization would bring on problems of juvenile delinquency, alcoholism, racial conflict, the displacement of religion from the center of human existence, the increase in impersonal crime, and the demand for organized measures to cope with mentally ill human beings. No specialized social science was uniquely equipped to study these problems and provide advice to elite groups concerning their solution, so sociology grew up to perform these services.[16]

The ideas that sociology is (or should be) the master science of historical development, the study of the relations between the various specialized areas of human existence and the investigation of the leftovers from the other social sciences are merely a few of the multitude of suggested definitions of the scope of the discipline. It is important to note that none of these definitions is arbitrary, but that each one of them reflects the way that its proponents view human experience. For those who believe that experience is divided up into neat boxes, sociology will have a special scope distinguishing it clearly from the other social sciences. On the other hand, for those who view experience as a field, there will be no clear lines of demarcation between the disciplines.

Establishing Sociology as a Separate Discipline

One reason why a number of sociologists have been concerned to distinguish their discipline from the other social sciences is that sociology is one of the youngest human sciences. In the late nineteenth and early twentieth centuries, sociologists had to battle to gain their own departments and courses in the universities of the West.[17] They had to prove both that they represented a respectable science, that they were studying different contents, and were employing different methods than the existing disciplines. Their respectability was in doubt because some considered them to be social reformers while others thought of them as propagandists for the establishment. These attacks were probably one reason why many sociologists bent over backwards to prove that they were like natural scientists. Even more serious were the fears of scholars in the other social sciences. Some historians felt threatened by a discipline that appeared to cover the same ground as their own field. They argued that no new discipline was necessary to investigate human affairs comprehensively, and remained unimpressed by claims that historians could content themselves with describing unique events while sociologists would search for general laws of human behavior.[18] Meanwhile, political scientists, anthropologists, and economists were busy making their claims to represent the most significant "science of man." In such a competitive and hostile environment it is no wonder that sociologists felt called upon to prove that they had a specific and unique contribution to make to the advancement of human knowledge. Of course, they were unable to agree upon a common definition of the nature of that contribution.

The history of sociology shows clearly that other considerations than the quest for understanding frequently influence scholarly work. Like labor unions fighting jurisdictional battles and then reaching agreements about which trade does which work, academic disciplines have parcelled out human experience only after conflicts—often bitter ones. Definitions of scope have been used as weapons in such conflicts, with the more powerful disciplines making extravagant claims about the extent of their scope and the weaker disciplines making modest claims with the hope that they will be granted some niche in the academic marketplace. Thus, in its early years, sociology was a weak discipline that had to prove that it deserved a place in the university structure. Today, however, it is no longer applying for admission and need not prove that it is distinct in its scope from the other social sciences.

The subject matter, or scope, given to sociology in this book is *human action*. This is a wide scope, but it is the only one that will support the quest for self-understanding and the only one that is consistent with the idea of experience as a dynamic and shifting field combining feelings, objects, relations, and creative processes. Even if they have not always been anxious to admit it, since the beginnings of their discipline sociologists have ranged over the entire scope of human action and have studied it with a variety of methods. Sociology has been the one discipline besides history to take a consistently comprehensive view of human experience. Thus, the broad definition of scope that we have given merely makes explicit what many other sociologists have known but have left unsaid.

Human action is a process interrelating groups, relations, objects, and purposes. In its briefest definition, a full human action is a group of people in relation to one another, using a set of objects for the realization of purposes. It is not easy to grasp the whole meaning of this definition all at once, but certain points are relatively apparent. First, our account of human action does not have for its basis a single individual doing something. In fact, for the moment, the "individual" is left out of the description altogether. Instead of the common-sense way of thinking about action as proceeding from particular "actors" (individuals) sociologists think about action in a group setting. However, it would be a mistake to think that sociologists simply substitute the unit group for the individual and then go on to state that action proceeds from a group "will" or a group "mind." According to the sociological view of action, there is no group will or group mind. Rather, groups are only evident where human beings are in relation to one another and using objects to realize purposes. There are no groups apart from these activities, and it would not be inaccurate to say that the extent of the activity defines the extent of the group. For example, the group of undergraduate sociology students does not have a will or a mind of its own, but is defined by the activities involved in being a sociology student, such as registering for courses, taking examinations, listening to lectures, participating in discussions, and reading books and articles. What sense would it make to say that there was a group will standing behind these activities and determining them? Yet there are people who believe that such groups as the "American people" or the "black people" have destinies and "souls" which in some way can be separated from concrete activities.

A second point following from the definition of human action is that, among other things, the group is a network of relations. Among some sociology students there is competition for grades and among others there is cooperation in attempting to understand the human condition. In certain cases there is competition and cooperation going on at the same time. Sometimes, even among sociology students, there is outright conflict, as when someone with a revolutionary vision of the human condition encounters someone whose vision emphasizes the goodness of the present order. The relations that occur in the process of human action are sometimes fixed in advance by rules, sometimes they seem to arise spontaneously and sometimes they grow up around systems of rules, subverting these systems or reinforcing them. Often the people involved in the relations are not aware of them, as when professors in college are not aware that they are competing with one another for the student's time. Frequently the individual has little or no control over the relations in which he is enmeshed. Does the student preparing to enter graduate school have control over the competitive relation governing the distribution of the limited number of places and the limited amount of financial aid available? Whether he likes it or not, if he is seeking to enter graduate school he is engaged in a competition with others having similar purposes. This lack of control by individuals over many of the relations that they enter is another indication of why sociologists do not begin with the individual in their account of human action.

A third aspect of the definition of human activity also takes one beyond the individual. Interrelated group activities refer to meaningful objects available to a number of actors. Perhaps the most striking feature of human action is the one that is usually most taken for granted—the fact that the human world is a world of meaning.[19] For the most part, experience does not appear as a meaningless blur, but as a relatively well ordered array of objects linked to one another in significant relations. It is culture that makes this order possible. A cultural object is a human creation with a usage attached which, if used in the prescribed way, will provoke a relatively standardized experience. Examples of cultural objects are tools, rules, symbols, and products. A hammer used correctly will allow one to pound a nail into a piece of wood, a set of rules followed by a group of people will create a particular social situation, a word whose meaning is known will allow one to recall past events and tell others about them, a television set when properly adjusted will allow one to witness the evening news. Hammers, the rules of parliamentary procedure, words, and television sets are all cultural objects. They are human creations that can be used over and over again to provoke standardized experiences.

The Sweep of Culture

When it is grasped, the imposing character of culture is very impressive. Any single individual is responsible for only the tiniest fragment of the objects available in the field of experience. A person's innermost thoughts are drenched in culture, because they are expressed in words that he has learned from others, rather than in symbols that he has thought up himself. The ways of processing and preparing the foods that he eats to sustain life are parts of culture and were not put into being by his individual activity. The systems for making decisions that he encounters when he is involved in disputes were in the process of development long before he was born. The very things that he finds beautiful are usually the creations of others and, at the very least, were identified by others long ago. It would be possible to go on endlessly pointing out how dependent human beings are upon culture. In most phases of existence, individual persons are far more representatives of culturally defined processes than they are freely creative actors. The genius at the game of chess, the master carpenter, the assembly-line worker, the housewife and mother are all representatives of a long history of cultural development. Perhaps the chess master adds his own individualized flair to the game, but he works within rules that he did not devise, he learned how to play from others, and he has usually studied the styles of the great masters of the past.

The immense, massive, and imposing character of culture is normally taken for granted in everyday life. People talk about "their" automobiles, "their" houses, "their" children. They forget that they only acquired the automobiles and the houses because others first designed and produced them, still others financed them, and yet others recognize rights of ownership. They forget that the ways in which they raise their children are not original, but were usually devised long ago. In short, they do not see themselves as mere points for the organization of culture. Perhaps one important reason why the significance of culture is generally ignored is that much of it seems to take care of itself. Most people, for example, do not worry continually about the language that they use in everyday life. They are not afraid that tomorrow the English language will not be understood. They expect that people will continue to give and receive messages in English and that children will continue to be taught the language. They only begin to worry about the language when they are confronted with specific problems.[20] For example, they will become concerned if people who should "know better" persist in misunderstanding them. The importance of language will come home to them when they are in contact with people who cannot speak English, or refuse to do so. They may become enraged when specialists insist upon speaking to them in words that they cannot understand. They may feel helpless and inadequate if they "cannot find the words" to describe the way they feel or to describe something unique that they have observed. Thus, people will begin to see the importance of culture when they are confronted with its inadequacies or when they have problems using it. However, such insights into the significance of culture are almost never carried over to a durable awareness of the person's dependence upon culture as a whole. Problems with language, for example, occur *within the context* of a given language. The context itself is normally not questioned, merely the specific thing that is responsible for the problem. Similarly, when a television set breaks down, it is usually not the entire system of electrification and electrical appliances which is brought into question, but merely a faulty circuit board.

In order to undertake the process of self-understanding, it is necessary for a person to wrench himself out of the everyday way of looking at the world and into a wider perspective that looks upon human action. Ordinarily, people look at themselves as the centers of the human universe and look at culture as organized around them. Rather than seeing themselves as representatives of long lines of historical development and as participants in complex chains of action beyond the grasp of any single person, they see themselves as the causes of human events. It is just this way of looking at things, of course, that makes a person most the slave of culture. People who believe that they are at the center of human affairs are unlikely ever to question the cultural context in which they are embedded.[21] They will believe that their most important activities are "natural" and could not be otherwise. They will believe that "God speaks in English," in the sense that any thought worth expressing can be expressed in the English language, and that "children need a mother at home if they are going to grow up to be normal." Thus, the people who are the staunchest individualists can at times also be the most abject slaves to culture. Their very individualism is part of a long tradition in Western economic and political life.[22] Conversely, the quickest way for a person to become free is to recognize his dependence on culture. Through such recognition he will be able to scrutinize the cultural context in which he is embedded, see its strengths and limitations, and compare it to other contexts. This is the idea behind the phrase "liberal education." For example, it has been a traditional goal of liberal education that people learn a language other than their native tongue. The reasoning is that learning another language will help allow one to gain a better understanding of communication. This understanding will be the result of clarification, generalization, and relativization with respect to language. Thus, liberal education, in its broadest sense, is carrying the process of self-understanding into as many areas of life as possible.

The importance of culture has been stressed so much in the preceding discussion because it is the key to understanding why the sociologist considers human action to be far wider than the movements of individual organisms. Awareness of culture has also been one of the primary means by which twentieth-century thinkers have liberated themselves from the notion that the self is property and have been able to grasp the idea that the self is process. While the group takes action beyond the organism, it is still easy to think of the group not as a field of activity but as a set of organisms. While the idea of relation brings home the interdependence of human beings, it is still easy to think of relations as happenings between two concrete organisms rather than as processes through which activities are interlaced. Similar evasions are more difficult to make with respect to culture, because culture is the content being organized by groups in their interrelated activities.

Bentley's Concepts of Space One of the most illuminating descriptions of the way in which culture opens out human action beyond the individual was done by Arthur F. Bentley.[23] Bentley's concern was to reveal the idea of space adequate to describing human activity precisely. While this problem appears to be somewhat abstract and removed from the quest for self-understanding, it has close connections with the major themes of this book. By following Bentley through the various ways in which space can be conceived in sociology, one will be able to make the transition from the everyday perspective to the sociological perspective.

The first idea of space discussed by Bentley is "movement-space." There are two varieties of movement-space. The crudest description of movement-space confines the description of human affairs to events that take place inside of the biological organism, such as nerve impulses. Restricting space this narrowly means that the sociologist could never account scientifically for his own activity of selecting a problem for investigation, observing relevant phenomena and reporting his results. A wider movement-space than the inside of the organism is the space formed by body movements. Many sociologists claim to use this space in their research when they state that they are studying "observable human behaviors." However, confining oneself to body movements creates a problem for the sociologist. Sheer body movements have no meanings in themselves. Is waving a clenched fist a sign of anger, a sign of the unity of a group, a greeting, or something else? The answer to this question cannot be determined by studying the body movement itself and confining one's observations to movement-space. Noting this difficulty, Bentley argues that there must be an idea of space adequate to take meanings into account.

The second idea of space discussed by Bentley is "action-space." Here, space is no longer defined by successive body movements, but is defined by the entire field of activity taken up by an organism over time.[24] Action-space is what most people assume in their everyday lives when they describe activities. They begin thinking of space as the field that they use for carrying out their daily activities, and then extend this notion to viewing space as a great container in which things go on. However, close inspection shows that action-space is not adequate for describing human activities. First, it is obvious that human organisms do not occupy action-spaces distinctly separate from one another. There is a great degree of overlap among action-spaces, and what accounts for this overlap is that human beings are engaged in common activities. For the most part, these activities are organized around complexes of cultural objects, such as factories and homes, rather than around biological organisms. Second, the extent of action-space seems to vary with the activity being performed rather than with any state of the organism. When a person goes off to college his action-space changes, not as a result of his organism changing, but as a result of his undertaking a new activity. Thus, Bentley argues that it is putting the cart before the horse to speak in terms of action-space. The space taken up by human events is not the sum of a number of action-spaces but, instead, action-spaces are merely the results of human activities.

Bentley's idea of a space adequate for describing human affairs is an attempt to overcome the weaknesses in the notions of movement-space and action-space. His "transactional space" is neither defined by body movements nor by the field taken up by an organism's activity, but by activities themselves in their spread over time and space. Thus, the activity of making automobiles has a certain spread that defines its transactional space. This spread is already longer than any single individual's lifespan, and wider than any single individual's comprehension (like the unification of France over several centuries). By adopting transactional space as his frame of reference, the sociologist is able to add an historical depth and a comparative breadth to his work. Bentley would argue that, whenever people have given accurate, consistent, adequate and fruitful accounts of human affairs, they have assumed the framework of transactional space whether or not they were aware of doing so. For example, somebody describing the development of the automobile industry and its consequences for the existence of organization does not conduct his analysis in terms of the particular action-spaces of specific individuals who have at one time or another produced or used automobiles. Rather, he considers the transactional space taken up by activities engaged in with respect to automobiles. He does not look at particular action-spaces both because they will overlap with one another in many cases and because they will contain much that is not relevant to his problem. Of course, if someone's concern is describing the activities of organisms, action-space is the appropriate notion of space to use. It is well to ask, however, whether human beings can be considered fruitfully merely as "behavioral organisms" or whether serious inquiry into the human condition demands that action be considered in its wider space and time spread.

Transactional space is the frame in which human action, as the sociologist considers it, occurs. In transactional space, cultural objects and the activities undertaken with respect to them are the center of attention, rather than individuals. These activities always involve groups, at the very least in the sense that for a cultural object to exist it must have a sharable meaning and the possibility of being available to more than one human being. Most cultural objects involve groups to a far greater extent, in the sense that they can be neither produced, used, managed, nor known without the involvement of a number of people. Similarly, the activities that take up transactional space always involve relations, in the sense that group activity is the interlacing of human relations. Producing, using, managing, and knowing all involve, at one time or another, one or more of such relations as cooperation, competition, conflict, love and exchange. By removing oneself from action-space and placing oneself in transactional space, one is enabled to appreciate a process of human action extending far beyond any particular individual and even beyond any specific membership group.

The discussion of groups, relations, and cultural objects as phases of human action, prepares the way for the fourth point contained in the definition of action. A full human action was defined before as a group of people in relation to one another, using a set of objects for the realization of purposes. The notions of group, relation, and object all take one away from the person as central focus. The idea of purpose reinstates the person into the process of human action.

The Purposefulness of Culture While insight into the immensity of culture allows one to appreciate the dependence of human beings on a wide field of activity, it becomes at some point necessary to account for the existence of this humanized cultural world. Some sociologists have attempted to view culture as a "thing" which somehow determines human beings to act in preordained ways. According to this viewpoint, the person is a resultant of the intersection of the "organic" (biology) and the "superorganic" (cultural object).[25] From where, however, does this superorganic realm arise? A restrictive empiricist might argue that culture is a means by which human beings secure their biological survival as a species. While this may be a result of culture, it is quite difficult to show that all cultural objects have this consequence and even more difficult to show that all cultural objects are direct responses to the drive towards survival (if there is such a drive at all). An expansive empiricist, who is not tied down to movement-space as a frame of reference, need not reduce "culture" to "nature." Rather, since he takes the entire domain of experience as his province, he can note that cultural objects are inserted into human existence through the creative and purposing activities of human beings.[26]

Just as human action has a spatial dimension, it also has a time dimension. This time dimension does not include only the past and the present, but also extends into the future. Human beings project images of the future ahead of themselves and then attempt to bring some of these visions into existence. This futuring activity is responsible for the insertion of new cultural objects into existence, as well as for the more mundane acts involved in achieving culturally given purposes.[27] For example, the chess master who devises a new strategy and then attempts to put it to work is inserting a new cultural object into existence. However, the more general purpose that he has of winning the match is culturally given.

Figure 5.2. WAYS OF CONCEIVING SPACE

Movement-Space:	The space taken up by a particular body movement (e.g., the wave of an arm)
Action-Space:	The space taken up by the actions of an organism (e.g., the office where a person works)

Socio-Cultural-Space: The space taken up by human projects (e.g., all the places where this book was written, produced, read, etc.)

A Sociologist's View of Time A description of time parallel to Bentley's analysis of space can be developed to make more sense out of evolving human purpose. The most restricted frame of time is "movement-time" confined to present body processes or sucessive body movements. In this notion of time there is no idea of proceeding in a meaningful way from the present into the future. There is merely the notion that at a certain instant a certain movement took place. Movement-time sees human activity as a series of "presents" detached from one another. No attention is given to the fact that accumulated past experiences make a difference for present action.

A wider frame of time is "action-time," which takes account of the summed-up life history of the organism. The framework of action-time carries the recognition that human beings are continually accumulating fresh experiences and, to some degree or other, integrating them with past experiences. Each organism is a unique center for the integration of experience and, according to sociologists who use action-time, memory of past events is a key factor in shaping the course of present activity.[28] The common expression, "His past has come back to haunt him," shows recogntion of the importance of action-time in human existence. Just as action-space spread out to include the organism's activities, so action-time spreads out to include the organism's life history. However, while action-time has distinct advantages over movement-time, it is not adequate to describing human activity, because it does not contain a necessary future reference.

A notion of transactional time can be developed to remedy the deficiencies of movement-time and action-time. Transactional time expands the frame of time to include the future perspectives of human beings. Not only are human beings the organizers and integrators of present and past experiences; they are also the creators of the future through their decisions to carry on or alter ongoing activities in the name of projected purposes. Thus, human activity is prospective (forward-looking) as well as retrospective (backward-looking). Human beings are enmeshed in a web of groups, relations, and cultural objects, but present activities carry with them a future reference. It is through this future reference that human beings are enabled to reject the propagandist's claim that "things are as they have to be." It is also to this future reference that Gurvitch referred when he stated that human experience breaks without cease its own frames of reference. An appropriate motto for the sociologist using action-time would be, "Where there is life there is hope." The sociologist using a transactional perspective would have to deny this and say instead, "Where there is hope there is human activity."

Figure 5.3. WAYS OF CONCEIVING TIME

        Movement-Time: The time elapsed in a particular body movement
              Action-Time: The lifetime of an organism
   Socio-Cultural-Time: The time of human projects—past, present, and future

Note the similarity to the ways of conceiving space in Figure 5.2.

Thus, the idea of purpose brings the person back into human action, not as the fundamental unit of analysis which "causes" everything to happen, but as the focus of purposive activity and as the gateway through which human activity enters the future. What purposes could there be without groups, relations, and cultural objects? Purposes have reference to activities involving a number of people, they relate to other purposes in a number of ways, and they are expressed in terms of plans for cultural objects. Yet what would groups, relations, and cultural objects be without purposes? There might be packs of organisms reproducing themselves in an endless cycle and changing only in response to changes in climate and vegetation, and to mutations in their germ cells. There might be blind and predetermined relations of conflict or collaboration, as in "wars" between armies of ants or in the feeding of the queen ant by worker ants in a single colony. There would not be cultural objects, because for these to reach their full development they must be designed to realize a purpose. There might, however, be such structures as beaver dams, made by organisms following a biologically determined program. In short, there could be life without purpose, but no human existence. There could be action-space and action-time, but no transactional space and time.

Figure 5.4. THE PHASES OF HUMAN ACTION

              Group: People are observed acting together.
         Relation: People interact with one another cooperatively, competitively, in conflict, and with love.
   Cultural object: People act with respect to objects which have meaning for them.

Purpose: People act from motives and for goals.

A human act is a group of human beings, in relation to each other, oriented toward meaningful objects and entertaining purposes. Fighting a war and making love are examples of human actions.

Humanistic sociology is the study of human action in its fullest extent. It is not "humanistic" because it idealizes the individual, preaches the love of humanity, recognizes the emotional element in human existence, or commits itself to equality among classes, races and sexes.[29] It is humanistic because of its expansive empiricism, which takes account of the full range of experience and the complete extent of the process of action in time and space. The major idea of humanistic sociology is that the process of human action is far wider than the activity of any particular individual or group. This means that the human condition cannot be understood by describing it in terms of the needs or desires of individuals, or with reference to the interests or demands of groups. Both groups and individuals are aspects of activity, rather than entities or "things" standing behind activity and "causing" it to happen. Think for a moment about what you call your own activity. Have you ever found yourself completely at rest and then pushed a button to get yourself moving in a particular direction? Not if your experience has been at all like ours. We find ourselves acting whether we like it or not. Even when we are sleeping we have dreams. When we are fortunate enough to integrate our various activities, thoughts, and feelings into some kind of unity and thereby exert some control over them, we consider it quite an achievement, if only a temporary achievement.[30] Continuous organization and reorganization of existence is the price that people pay for having a future reference to activity. It is also the reward for being human.

Figure 5.5. TYPES OF HUMAN ACTIONS

Creative Acts:	The meaning of the act is unknown until the act is completed (e.g., the composition of a new song).
Imitative Acts:	The meaning of the act is known consciously throughout the act (e.g., practicing a dance step which one has been taught).
Habitual Acts:	The act is touched off by an external stimulus and is performed without thought (e.g., brushing your teeth in the morning . . . if you are in the habit).

A full human action includes groups, relations, objects and purposes. However, all human actions do not combine these components in the same way. Florian Znaniecki has distinguished among creative, reproductive, and habitual actions: "Creative actions, reproductive (imitative) actions, and habitual actions differ mainly in the formation of their purposes. At one limit we find creative actions in which the purpose continues to evolve until the action is completed. At the other limit, we observe habitual actions, in which the purpose is formed at the very moment when the action starts. In between these limits fall imitative actions, in which stabilization of the purpose is achieved during the first part of the action and the purpose remains unchanged during its realization."[31] At the limit of habitual actions, future reference is at its minimum and human beings appear to behave like trained animals. The propagandist's dream would be to have all human action except the elite's become habitual and to be directed toward serving the elite's interests. One of the moral purposes of the sociologist is to expand the range of creative actions. However, the sociologist understands very well that, for creative actions to be more than childish play, they must be based on a disciplined appreciation of existing cultural objects. This means that the route to creative freedom involves making a large number of activities habitual and spending a great deal of one's life performing imitative actions. Many actions which are first imitative are usefully made habitual once they are learned. For example, what good would it be to deliberate about how to brush your teeth every morning? And, of course, the destiny of creative actions is to be made imitative. We are relieved that we were not called upon to reinvent the typewriter before beginning work on this book.

Understanding human action as a process involving groups, relations, objects and purposes saves one from the oversimplifications of worshiping such abstractions as "society" or the "individual" or "culture." The problem of human action is not deciding whether one should favor the "individual" over "society" or sacrifice individual rights to the collective good. Rather, it is a problem of which actions should be encouraged and which ones discouraged. It is, of course, also a problem of how actions can be effectively encouraged and discouraged, and how diverse actions can be organized into a harmonious whole. While these problems are far from solution, they are at least far more intelligible than the older dilemmas.

EXPERIENCE AND ACTION

The basis of a humanistic sociology is expansive empiricism. As opposed to restrictive empiricism, which limits sociologists to studying observable behavior, expansive empiricism permits sociologists to investigate the full range of human experience. A comprehensive view of human experience contains the elements of lived experience, or the life of feeling, social experience, or the processes of relation among human actions, cultural experience, or the experience of blocked-off and definable objects, and creative experience, or the very processes of change. None of these types of experience is shut off from the others by fixed boundaries. Rather, experience is a dynamic field, continually moving in the direction of one or another type of experience, but always including elements of all four.

Given a basis of expansive empiricism, the scope of sociology is the process of human action. Human action, from a sociologist's perspective, should not be confused with the behaviors of particular individuals or concrete groups. Rather, it is a process spreading out in space and time far beyond the range of specific individuals or groups. The process of human action contains the four components of group, relation, cultural object and purpose. The definition of a full human action is a group of people in relation to one another, using a set of objects for the realization of purposes. This view of human action assumes definitions of space and time that treat space as a field taken up by activity, rather than as an area circumscribed by body motion or the behavior of an organism, and of time as a process extending from the past into the future, rather than as a series of instants or the life history of an organism.

Expansive empiricism and the full human action define a humanistic sociology, which is distinguished not by its good intentions toward humanity, but by its willingness to investigate all facets of human experience without preconceived notions.

6

SOCIOLOGY AS A COMMITMENT

In the preceding chapter human action was distinguished as the scope, or subject matter, of sociology. We define human action as a process interrelating groups, relations, objects, and purposes. As actors, sociologists do not stand apart from other human beings in any significant respect. They can use the findings and methods of sociology to gain awareness of and insight into themselves, or they can resist the application of sociology to their own lives. Spurred on by the social divisions that became apparent in the "liberation movements" of the 1960s, sociologists have become increasingly concerned with the critical examination of themselves and their discipline. In one of the most important and penetrating works of the 1960s, *The Coming Crisis of Western Sociology*, Alvin Gouldner calls self-confrontation by sociologists "reflexive sociology": "A reflexive sociology means that we sociologists must—at the very least—acquire the ingrained *habit* of viewing our own beliefs as we now view those held by others."[1] It "requires that sociologists cease acting as if they thought of subjects and objects, sociologists who study and 'laymen' who are studied, as two distinct breeds of men."[2] "Insofar as social reality is seen as contingent in part on the effort, the character, and the position of the knower, the search for knowledge about social worlds is also contingent upon the knower's *self-awareness.*"[3]

Reflexive sociology, or the process of self-understanding directed by sociologists at themselves, can only be practiced by investigating the contexts in which sociologists work. The sociologist need not be considered merely as a scientific investigator attempting to understand or explain human activity; he may also be viewed as someone occupying a specific organizational position, as someone whose work may be beneficial to some social groups and harmful to others. The very "products" that sociologists "manufacture" (the body of knowledge known as sociology) may be influenced in form and content by the investigator's own social position and by the demands of clients or employers. Like any other human beings, sociologists can undertake the processes of clarification, generalization, relativization, and commitment. They can identify their goals, the groups that share them, and the relations of these groups to others; and then they can commit themselves to a course of action. We view the most significant contexts of sociologists as the university, the discipline, and the research-granting organization. This judgment follows from our commitment to a "process" theory of society, which holds that the processes of organizing human activity are more significant than any particular content, such as economic or political activity.[4] Other sociologists, who adhere to monistic economic theories, have identified different contexts as the most relevant. For example, Dusky Lee Smith and Herman and Julia Geshwender view the economic structure of corporate capitalism as the crucial context determining the work of the founders of American sociology.[5]

THE MULTIVERSITY

The university is perhaps the most significant context for sociologists. The vast majority of practicing sociologists are employed by institutions of higher learning, and practically all sociologists have been trained in them. Although a few small private liberal arts colleges remain, the university, like other sectors of mass society, has tended toward bigness and conglomeration. Since World War II, vast educational organizations, which Clark Kerr has called "multiversities," have appeared.[6] Kerr, a former president of the University of California, used the term to refer to such contemporary universities as his own, ones that are massive in size and interpenetrate with the major complexes of interest groups in mass society. Nevertheless, the mere size of the multiversity, with tens of thousands of students and hundreds of faculty members, is one of its least significant characteristics. More important is the vast array of activities that take place under its umbrella. One multiversity with which we are familiar hosts conferences for plumbers, future farmers, and a variety of other nonacademic groups; owns and operates three golf courses and a hotel; sells apples grown in its horticultural farms; runs a radio station; fields basketball and football teams that often draw 70,000 or more spectators to contests; sponsors rock and classical music concerts by nationally known artists; and owns and leases dozens of private homes.

The units of the multiversity are frequently at cross purposes with one another, and the principle governing what is to be undertaken is growth in human and material "resources." Robin Williams states that "the actual goals of university administrators are to increase the wealth, size, and public renown of their institutions."[7] Richard Fallenbaum, writing in a collection of essays on the student revolt at Kerr's Berkeley campus, states: "Many university undertakings are valuable but many others are ridiculous and even dangerous. The only quality that is common to them all is that they increase the university's size and prestige."[8]

One should not get the impression that this growth is merely random. As an integral part of mass society, the multiversity's expansion is consonant with the wealth, power, and prestige of other major institutions. Specialized and technical training has supplanted the liberal arts education, thereby providing existing bureaucracies with professional and semiprofessional personnel. When the Soviet Union's launching of the Sputnik satellite wounded American pride in 1957, science departments in the multiversity immediately swelled and produced armies of scientists and engineers. The World War II baby boom, coupled with increased industrial desire for college-trained personnel, created a demand for more college teachers. Existing graduate departments at the multiversity stepped up their "productivity," and undergraduate departments added masters or doctoral programs.[9] In addition to furthering the process of specialization and cultivating the professional mentality, some critics have pointed out that the multiversity encourages students to become acquiescent consumers of mass entertainments. A former Berkeley graduate student wrote in an open letter to undergraduates: "The multiversity is the slickest appeal ever made for you to fortify your organization-man mentalities, for you to lead privatized lives in which it is a virtue for you to go greedily 'on the make.' "[10]

The academic departments of the multiversity reflect in miniature the context in which they are located. As in mass society in general, the hierarchy of authority is not coincident with technical competence. Indeed, members of a given department often have only the vaguest notion of the research activities of a colleague, because areas of specialization tend to be defined in terms of airtight, mutually exclusive compartments. Mirroring the different schools and departments are separate and jealously guarded fiefdoms within departments, and factions battle with one another for space, students, monies, and prestige. Frequently, the enclaves of power are supported by agencies outside the multiversity, especially through research or development grants.[11] The multiversity's fragmentation of human experience into unrelated bits through grants of departmental autonomy is intensified by the department's subdivision of its discretion into smaller specialized bits doled out to individual professors. The fragmentation of sociological knowledge into airtight compartments, in which a vision of the whole enterprise of sociology and of the individual is lost, is quite in keeping with the context of the multiversity.

Teaching still is an activity within the multiversity, but it differs significantly from teaching in smaller colleges. The class size is larger: introductory lecture courses rarely have fewer than fifty students and frequently have several hundred. And although the multiversities vie with one another to get the top people in each discipline, the published and nationally recognized professor does little teaching. In many instances the academic celebrity does no teaching at all. Clark Kerr claims that the "mark of a university 'on the make' is a mad scramble for football stars and professional luminaries. The former do little studying and the latter little teaching, and so they form a neat combination of muscle and intellect."[12] Teaching is viewed as a chore to be delegated to others. The stars concentrate on research and consulting.

Opportunities abound in all disciplines for consulting, which is often handsomely paid for by governmental agencies and various business enterprises. Sociologists, depending on their orientation and specialty, can consult for such diverse agencies and organizations as the Bureau of the Census, the Department of the Navy, correctional institutions, hospitals, all types of business concerns, textbook publishers, and so on. The more grants obtained and publications garnered (these are the necessary credentials for consulting work as well as for pay raises and promotion in rank), the less the teaching load. Who, then, does the teaching?

As many of the readers of this book are aware, the lion's share of the teaching is done by young and inexperienced professors and graduate assistants. This, of course, does not mean that the teaching is of low quality or any worse than it would be if a noted professor conducted the class. An older academician who is unpublished finds no opportunities in the multiversity. Such a person often winds up at a small college or goes into business or government work related to his field of specialization. As for graduate teaching assistants, they often find it difficult to take their duties seriously because their professors view teaching as a chore or a punishment. And the career advancement of those graduate students who go on to positions in the multiversity will not be dependent upon the quality of their teaching. The relative unimportance of communicating sociological understanding through teaching in the multiversity corresponds to the type of sociology that cannot be used by individuals in their everyday lives.

The academic setting has traditionally been a center not only for teaching but also for the "production" of knowledge. Prior to the emergence of mass society, research was not the primary purpose of professors, but was made possible through the provision of space and equipment by the colleges (laboratories and libraries, for example). In addition, there frequently was an appreciative audience present, composed of colleagues and sometimes students who were able to understand and evaluate research work. The production of knowledge in the multiversity is far more complex than it was in the college, due in part to the extreme specialization characteristic of every field of inquiry. Research is often carried on in hierarchically ordered teams, but even when it is done by a solitary scholar, equipment costs are too high to be borne by the institution. Tuition accounts for a minor part of the multiversity's income.[13] Professors attempt to obtain backing for their research from public or private foundations. Such "grants" include an overhead charge, usually about 50 percent of the funds, in payment to the university for released teaching time and office space. The high degree of specialization limits the possibilities for a local appreciative audience. At their best, scholarly journals and meetings sponsored by disciplinary associations serve to bring together appreciative audiences.

EXERCISE

In what ways does the school that you attend have the characteristics of a multiversity? Has the specific institutional context had an influence on your education?

Paradigms

The dominant myth about sociological research (as well as that done in all other fields) is that scholars are not influenced by their social and cultural contexts. This position was elaborated by Max Weber, who claimed that the social sciences should and could be value free.[14] Alvin Gouldner deftly critiques this view and indicates how useful it is for those who espouse it.[15] Among other uses, the belief in value neutrality justifies the sale of one's talents to the highest bidder. Much of the research carried on in the multiversity is very expensive and is funded largely through government, business, and private foundations such as the National Science Foundation, IBM, and the Rockefeller Foundation, respectively. None of the funds are "clean" in the sense that, whether they are for "basic" or "applied" research, they do not tie the researcher to some complex of interest groups. Frequently, researchers speak of the happy coincidence through which the problems they always wanted to work on are the ones for which funds are provided. Such good luck occurs too often for such protestations to be taken seriously.

The content and form of sociological research are influenced by many factors including the system of rewards in the multiversity and the desires of the organizations granting the funds. The status system within the discipline rewards those who choose problems and methods that are "in vogue" and penalizes those whose work is considered passé. According to prevailing mythology, the state of scientific knowledge within the profession is supposed to dictate what questions are relevant for guiding one's research, one's ideological commitments, and one's personal interests. The most widespread hypothesis held by sociologists about how the content of research is chosen is that questions are generated by "paradigms." In his influential book *The Structure of Scientific Revolutions*, Thomas Kuhn defines a paradigm as "a universally recognized scientific achievement that for a time provides model problems and solutions to a community of practitioners."[16] Paradigm guidance is at best a very partial explanation of problem selection, however. It does not account for why problems are selected that challenge the dominant paradigm and may eventually lead to what Kuhn calls "scientific revolutions" in which a new paradigm becomes predominant. Even more problematic is the issue of whether sociology with its plurality of approaches, traditions, perspectives, and methods can be seen to have anything akin to a paradigm.[17]

Increased self-awareness and sensitivity to the contexts of their work has affected sociologists in several ways. Such heightened awareness has led to a new subfield in the discipline called the "sociology of sociology." Some have found in it an opportunity for navel-contemplation and self-celebration, while others have discovered a mine of easily obtainable data and a new frontier in which it is possible to "crank out" innumerable little studies. Nevertheless, for those who have taken them seriously, reflexivity and self-understanding have widened the scope of sociologists' commitments and have given them a new sense of responsibility for the social and political consequences of their work.

PROPAGANDA MILLS

Another significant context within which the sociologist operates is that of a pluralist society in which numerous competitors define the human condition. As opposed to encouraging relativization and an understanding of one's own context, as does the best of sociology, commercial advertisers and political propagandists have as their purpose the destruction of the social context in order to leave the isolated self vulnerable to appeals to self-esteem and fear. Their object is to destroy independent judgment and to persuade individuals to buy a product or make a commitment to support a party or personality.

The activity of persuading people to make economic and political decisions with reference to nonrational criteria is one of the most highly differentiated and bureaucratized activities in mass society. People in the United States are sometimes frightened when they learn about the incessant political propaganda supporting the ruling elites in communist countries. They believe that it would be terrible to be assailed day in and day out by appeals to work harder to realize the five-year plan or to feel enraged at the bourgeois imperialists. Such propaganda seems the very antithesis of freedom. But these same people think nothing of being assailed by endless commercials for laxatives, deodorants, automobiles, floor polishes, beer, and various and sundry other products. They do not believe they have the right to demand freedom from sales pressure. Since salesmen are everywhere—on the radio and TV, in the newspapers and magazines, on billboards, over the telephone, on the doorstep, and in commercial establishments—people take them for granted as an inherent feature of the human condition. Underlying this complacency is the assumption that what goes on in one's mind most of the time is not really all that important. So what if one cannot stop a jingle advertising chewing gum from running through one's head for an entire day? Some other nonsense would, presumably, have been going through the mind instead. Nevertheless, it is important to realize that the careers of many people are devoted to implanting just such jingles in the mind, and trying to envision what one's mental life would be like in the absence of advertising and propaganda.

The advertising and propaganda bureaucracies are massive and complex. De Fleur, in a description of mass media as social systems, shows how closely advertising is connected with the rest of what appears on the media. He identifies as the first phase of the communications process "research." Organizations "devoted to *research*, to measuring the preferences of media audiences, or to various forms of market research provide information to those responsible for selecting the categories of content that will be distributed to the audience."[18] This is the kind of job for which many undergraduates in psychology and sociology are prepared. The work involves determining who buys what and why, so that the advertising message can be effective in raising sales. The second phase of the process involves selecting a "distributor" for the advertising. The propagandist must determine which kinds of programs, magazines, or what not are best adapted as vehicles and contexts for the advertising message—one would not advertise a feminine hygiene deodorant in a hunting magazine. Of course, the process goes much farther than such an obvious example, because advertisers and corporations sometimes develop TV series adapted to selling their product, or pass judgment on the kinds of articles appearing in magazines.

De Fleur translates this observation into antiseptic "sociological" language which, incidentally, shows how "value neutral" science contains its own biases: "To the audience, the research, and the distributing components, we may add the role system of the *producer* of content. This component's primary link is with the *financial backer* (or *sponsor*) component and with the distributor, from whom money is obtained and for whom various forms of entertainment content are manufactured."[19] A dyed-in-the-wool Marxist militant could not have made the point more clearly: the content of the mass media is *manufactured* not for the audience but for the sponsor, who is presumably bankrolling the news and entertainment industry for some reason other than charity.

EXERCISE

Watch several advertisements on television. In what ways do they try to persuade you to buy the product? What motives do they appeal to?

Finally, the key integrating component of the entire mass media social system is the advertising agency: "Linking the sponsor, distributor, producer, and research organization are the *advertising agencies.* Paid primarily by the sponsor, this component provides (in return) certain ideas and services. For the most part, it provides the distributor with advertising messages."[20] Where does the audience fit into this scheme? De Fleur remarks that the "relationship between audience and distributor seems at first to be mostly a one-way link." However, these mere appearances mask the true contribution of the audience in a mass society: the audience "does provide its *attention.*" In fact, De Fleur continues, it is "precisely the attention of the audience that the distributor is attempting to solicit": "He sells this 'commodity' (attention) directly to his financial backer or sponsor."[21] Thus, from the media's point of view, they are selling part of your mind to a sponsor. We now turn to how they do it.

EXERCISE

Write an advertisement trying to sell some product that you own. To which group are you appealing? What principles of persuasion are you using? In order to be effective, have you violated any principles of critical reason?

The Mass Mind

In order to sell products or gain supporters for political movements (or raise the status of an ethnic group, create converts for a religion, or build up the image of a voluntary association), propagandists appeal to a set of mental and emotional processes that can conveniently be called the "mass mind." The mass mind is not a description of how any particular human being thinks or feels throughout most of his existence, nor is it a description of some "group mind" which mysteriously governs the actions of individuals as well as their judgments and emotions. Rather, the mass mind

Sociology as a Commitment

describes the *image* of mental life held by propagandists. Some people may even approach conforming to this image, but this does not mean that they *must* continue to conform or that the propagandists can induce them to conform. By understanding how propagandists define the mass mind, one is enabled to choose whether or not one will become an easy mark for the advertisers.

Reflections about the mass mind did not begin with propagandists and advertisers, but with social critics and thinkers. This is to be expected because it is characteristic of propagandists and advertisers regularly to draw upon what people have created and discovered in other contexts rather than to develop anything for themselves. Thus, in the nineteenth century, the social critic Gustave LeBon systematized the principles of the mass mind in his study of crowd behavior. According to LeBon, the crowd was the distinctive social form in mass society. People had been thrown together into cities and had lost their traditional social controls, making them vulnerable to flights of irrationality.

For LeBon, the hallmark of crowds was the lack of deliberation before they took action and the lack of control during the performance of action. Crowds were subject to the sway of suggestion, because their members were incapable of critical reflection: "Any display of premeditation by crowds is in consequence out of the question. They may be animated in succession by the most contrary sentiments, but they will always be under the influence of the exciting causes of the moment. They are like leaves which a tempest whirls up and scatters in every direction and then allows to fall."[22] Crowds lack the characteristics of critical reason, particularly with regard to the suspension of judgment necessary for relativization: "The simplicity and exaggeration of the sentiments of crowds have for result that a throng knows neither doubt nor uncertainty. . . . A suspicion transforms itself as soon as announced into incontrovertible evidence."[23]

It is important to note that the characteristics of the mass mind do not appear only in concrete groups of individuals given the name "crowds." Throughout mass society, often in the most rule-bound organizations, there is evidence of the crowd behavior identified by LeBon. Traits such as suggestibility, destructiveness, emotionality, and lack of self-control frequently appear in conglomerate organizations when the normal routine is disturbed by power struggles among administrators, demands by militant client groups, threats from other organizations, or factional struggles among competing cliques of specialists. Groups of professionals in bureaucracies may come to behave as crowds when they are cross-pressured or mobilized by authorities. Thus it is a mistake to look at crowd behavior and the mass mind as lower-class phenomena stemming from limited education and ineffective socialization. Rather, the appearance of crowds is encouraged by the power structure of mass society, which stresses top-down hierarchical authority of administrators. When this authority is questioned, those who have depended upon it to function routinely are frequently left without a focus for their activity and become open to the processes of suggestion and manipulation. Thus, crowd behavior is less a consequence of individual and cultural traits than an aspect of social organization. Further, crowd behavior may be one of the few effective means for stimulating social change in the hands of poorly organized and dispossessed social groups. It may, in fact, be a way of precipitating more coherent, responsible, and participative social action.

This possible function of crowds as agents of change, however, does not eliminate the unreflective character of their behavior. Ultimately, the way to diminish crowd behavior and the mass mind is to lessen the dependence of people on hierarchical power structures and to distribute societal resources in such a way that there are no dispossessed groups. In the absence of a more egalitarian social order, individuals can avoid being drawn into the cycle of suggestion and manipulation by applying the process of self-understanding and joining with others in strong informal organizations critical of power structures and capable of self-defense and opposition when these structures undergo their frequent and recurrent breakdowns. It is useful to distinguish between crowds that appear when there is a breakdown in authority, and crowds that are manipulated by elites for ulterior purposes. The first type is a possible agent of social change acting against elites, while the second is an attempt by elites to exploit discontent to secure their position. In either case, though, the crowd is *reactive* rather than *constructive*, since constructive social action depends upon participants acting cooperatively to realize values to which they are committed.

The most striking instances of crowds are those that gather in the same action space and time during periods of social unrest, and that engage in violent or destructive activities. As LeBon was careful to point out, however, most crowds in mass society exist in sociocultural space and time, their members being out of eye- and earshot of one another. When a wave of patriotic intensity sweeps through the lower-middle classes of a nation, as, for example, when policemen begin putting flag decals on their cruisers and wearing flag patches on their uniforms; stores begin offering free flags along with purchases of appliances; women begin wearing red, white, and blue dresses; and people are arrested with some frequency for showing "disrespect" for the flag; a crowd is present just as surely as if a mob were storming a prison with the intent of freeing all the inmates.

Of course, crowds that exist in sociocultural space and time only, and not in action space and time, are vulnerable to intensive manipulation by small elites, which channel their passion into longer-term projects for gaining or maintaining advantage. For example, the owner of a department store who is concerned to increase sales may exploit patriotic fervor in order to draw people into his establishment. In some cases the elites may even be strong enough to create the very passion actuating the crowd. This may have taken place in the wave of working-class patriotism which arose in the late 1960s. The elites did not here create patriotism, nor were they personally responsible for the frustrations of many working men; but they did provide symbols, rationalizations, and reinforcements to the emerging crowd. The construction workers who rampaged through downtown New York in protest against longhairs and "peaceniks" had their arguments all ready for the television cameramen. In contrast, despite ceaseless efforts by organizations such as multinational oil companies to exploit patriotism during the celebrations of the Bicentennial of the American Revolution, a public suffering the effects of economic recession, inflation and shortages, and political scandal has not responded with zest to elite manipulation.

EXERCISE

Have you ever been a member of a crowd, taking on the characteristics of the mass mind? Describe your experience. How did you regain control over your judgment? If you do not believe that you have ever adopted the crowd mentality, how do you believe that you have avoided it?

STIMULUS-RESPONSE

Observations on crowd behavior can be generalized into a method for getting people to do things that they might not do if they applied critical reason. This is the method of association, or what is sometimes called behaviorism or stimulus-response. The method of association is the simplest form of manipulation and also far and away the most prevalent. When using this method, the propagandist links the activity he would like people to perform with some other object they desire or fear, or with some pleasant or unpleasant experience. For example, suppose the advertiser's plan is to have more people purchase a certain automobile. The simplest use of association would be to create billboards in which pretty girls and handsome men were clustered around the car, or in which the car appeared in a beautiful wooded glen. Here, the intent would be to have the viewer associate possession of the car with the experience of being with "beautiful" people, or with the experience of being in a beautiful environment. If successful, the advertiser will have manipulated the person looking at the billboard to buy the car because of the associations created by the advertiser. Thus the entire principle of association in advertising is to create a context for a product, which has nothing to do with the product itself, but which will favorably dispose the person to make a purchase.

What this means in terms of the image of mental life held by advertisers should be evident. Advertisers view human beings (including the readers of this book) as members of crowds who can be swayed into action by appeals having nothing to do with the action. How many times do you find yourself in a wooded glen with a car? Thus, association is the basic characteristic of the mass mind.

In order for association to work, the contexts in which propagandists place their products must be standardized and held constant. If people were continually rethinking their situations and reconstructing them, it would be impossible for advertisers to be sure that particular contexts would give rise to pleasant or unpleasant associations. There is nothing sacred about "youth" as a pleasant context. In some groups the aged are more highly esteemed than the young. Nevertheless, advertisers and political propagandists have exploited the context of youth so much in selling their products and policies that a group of young people having a good time (or "seriously" working toward social betterment) has become a standardized way of eliciting a pleasant emotional climate. The readers of this book might reflect for a moment about how closely the image of youth in commercials and political propaganda accords with the directly experienced quality of their own existence. The years between eighteen and twenty-five are frequently marked by uncertainty about the future, lack of confidence in one's capacities, fear that one is going to be dragged into a meaningless life, and relative poverty. Even more poignant than the middle-aged men and women in rock nightclubs are the young people who believe in the myths about themselves created by middle-aged propagandists.

Youth, of course, is merely one standardized context developed and exploited by advertisers and propagandists. Others are the suburban family, the back-slapping male peer group filled with "gusto," the wise wife concerned with the good of her husband and children, and the cute little old lady filled with a youthful zest for life. How does the little old lady look to the crippled old women who have nothing to do all day but watch TV in their nursing homes? She is not on TV for their benefit, but for ours—so that we can associate the product she is selling with eternal youthfulness.

In using the method of association, advertisers and propagandists take the product out of the context in which it will actually appear when consumed and put it into a contrived context that will fill it with pleasant or unpleasant (when the propaganda is designed to prevent action or stir up hatred) associations. How many husbands will go into transports of joy upon seeing that their wives have waxed the kitchen floor with a new product? Often they will not even notice that the floor has been waxed, and if their wives gently remind them, they may feel guilty rage about neglecting to comment. Since the basic method of advertising is association and catering to (and thereby fostering) the crowd mentality, debates about "truthfulness" in advertising and propaganda do not get to the heart of the matter. Advertisers often welcome the opportunity to tell the truth about their product or candidate (as long as they can select which part of the truth to tell), but they will not so easily give up the freedom to determine the context in which that truth will appear.

Other Characteristics of the Mass Mind

While suggestibility and the crowd mentality are the basic characteristics of the mass mind, other mental processes are assumed and exploited by advertisers and propagandists. One of the most important is the assumption that people have some sort of drive to be consistent and some desire to be right all the time.[24] For example, it is assumed (and to some extent can be shown to be true) that a person who purchases a consumer good, particularly one with a high price tag, will attempt to screen out anything unfavorable about that product and harp on everything good about it.[25] Of course, salesmen and politicians are always ready at hand to aid people in this process of accentuating the positive and eliminating the negative (called, in the antiseptic jargon of social psychology, "resolving cognitive dissonance"). Often the process of accentuating the positive is not even undertaken consciously, but is indulged in almost by habit. It becomes a method of manipulation when established authorities and spokesmen for powerful elites begin to emit propaganda emphasizing how important it is to look at the good side of things. They treat the nation in the same way that the auto salesmen treats the new car being brought back for major repairs; both claim that people should look at the positive aspects of the situation and not tear down a basically good thing.

Of course, there is an opposite form of manipulation, indulged in by some dissenters, which attempts to encourage discontent by accentuating the negative and eliminating the positive. And, naturally, both the apologist and the dissident rely upon fixed definitions of the "positive" and the "negative" to carry through their propaganda; they would go out of business quickly if people began to relativize their situations. However, it is unlikely that they will go out of business soon because they have been quite successful in fostering the mass mind and discouraging critical reflection—so successful, in fact, that some social psychologists believe that people "naturally" seek to live in a dream world of wishful thinking.[26]

The notion that people seek to resolve cognitive dissonance dovetails very well with the idea that people can be induced to act on the basis of pleasant or unpleasant associations. In resolving cognitive dissonance the person merely saves the propagandist the trouble of hiring good-looking women and famous athletes. Instead of being induced by a context created for him by the advertiser, the person creates his own wonderland of wooded glens and beautiful people, which then enslaves him to established commercial, political, appreciative, and educational organizations. People are continually in the process of creating their own contexts, most of which split them off from relations with others. A man, for example, may define his context as *his* family and *his* new house in the suburbs. The total vision of urban life evaporates for him, and the advertisers and propagandists are happy to assist in this evaporation. It is no wonder, then, that dissenters have a bad name throughout the world.

SOCIOLOGY AS COMMITMENT

An individual need not interpret life using a sociological perspective. Advertisers and propagandists provide an alternative vision of existence based on the categories of the mass mind in which critical judgment is suppressed. The initiation of the process of self-understanding and its broadening and deepening through the examination of theory, science, method, and action involve deliberate choices. Nobody can be forced to undertake sociological inquiry in the way that it has been defined in the preceding chapters. It is perhaps possible to torture and coerce a person into confessing to a crime he did not commit, but it is not possible to use torture and coercion to make an individual critically evaluate his image of the human condition.

Criticism and self-examination are processes that are internal to the person's consciousness. They cannot be observed directly by others, and only the individual knows with certainty whether or not they are going on. The effects of taking a sociological perspective may be observed in actual human relations in greater ability to consider divergent viewpoints and possibilities, and in greater strength to resist manipulation by authorities and elites. Apparent understanding of diversity and conflict often turns out to be a superficial façade of tolerance, however, and what seems to be firm resistance sometimes proves to be the transient consequence of blind resentment. A key factor that distinguishes human beings from other natural phenomena is the capacity for deception. A student may be trained to pass examinations through the rewards and punishments of the grading system, but such performance is no measure of a commitment to self-understanding.

There are two senses in which a person "chooses" sociology. First, one must decide whether or not to consider oneself in reference to a wider social and cultural context. All types of sociology reject the idea that the individual can be considered apart from groups, relational processes, and cultural objects. Those who believe that they are, or can be, independent of such influences have not chosen sociology; instead, they have decided to remain ignorant of the origins and consequences of their thoughts and actions. Second, once the individual has decided to take a sociological perspective, the choice remains of what kind of sociological inquiry to pursue. The idea that sociology is a process of self-understanding that involves the individual's personal encounter with multiple perspectives on the human condition is only one of many approaches to sociology. The other approaches also have their intelligent and dedicated adherents.

Anomie, Criticism, and "Everyday Life"

There is no universal agreement about either the possibility or the desirability of most people taking a sociological perspective. Many sociologists believe that the stability of human relations is based upon widespread and uncritical acceptance of "everyday life" or the "commonsense world." They hold that each social group has sets of expectations and rules that are "taken for granted" by its members. If enough people within the group begin to question and criticize these expectations and rules, some sociologists fear that the group will fall apart because those who compose it will no longer be able to rely upon one another to perform their appointed tasks and to respect each other's rights. Further, the individual who is caught up in such a situation may suffer *anomie* (a loss of standards for guiding action).[27] Such extreme doubt about what one should do and about the meaning of one's actions may result in the "acting out" of personal fantasies in public, and even in suicide.

Arguments against fostering a critical attitude toward social norms and relations go back at least as far in time as the beginnings of Western thought. The classical argument against universalizing the sociological perspective was offered by Plato in his *Republic*. Plato argued that even in the best society there would have to be a distinction between rulers and ruled. He believed that this distinction should be based on wisdom, but was confronted by the paradox that the majority of the unwise would not have sufficient knowledge to understand why the wise should rule. Plato resolved the problem by suggesting that the wise rulers should invent a myth to convince the majority that political inequality is right and proper.[28] While Plato actually justified political inequality by the demonstrated achievements of different people, he believed the majority should be told that inequality was due to the fact that individuals are innately different from one another: rulers are made of gold, soldiers of silver, and workers of bronze. Plato did not believe that the majority could understand and accept inequalities based upon achievement, but would only acquiesce in inequalities that were supposedly rooted in absolute and changeless differences.

In modern times myth has usually been defended by conservatives interested in supporting traditional privileges. For example, Edmund Burke argued that social life was made possible by widespread belief in "pleasing illusions," such as the idea that political authority is ordained by God and that the higher classes deserve their economic privileges.[29] Burke believed that effective criticism of pleasing illusions would lead to a brutal conflict over scarce resources and to tyranny unchecked by the moderating influences of custom and tradition.

Plato wrote in a society in which slavery went unquestioned, while Burke wrote in the wake of the French Revolution and saw his work as a warning against the dangers of mass democracy. Recent defenders of myths and pleasing illusions have written within mass democracies and, thus, have faced a problem that their predecessors did not encounter. The basic myth of mass democracy is that government should be "of the people, by the people, and for the people." How, then, is it possible to defend the restriction of critical awareness and self-understanding to a small number of specialists and leaders? Contemporary social thinkers who fear criticism cannot follow Plato and Burke and directly justify privilege, at least if they want to gain a wide hearing. They cannot argue that criticism will undermine elites, and therefore criticism is bad, because the people are supposed to determine what the elites do. Hence, they duck the question of inequality and privilege altogether and state that criticism and questioning destroy the solidity of "everyday life" and spread distrust and the loss of standards. Further, they argue that most people are not interested in examining their social and cultural contexts and should not be prodded into doing so. According to this line of argument, self-consciousness is not necessarily a blessing, and it may be a curse.[30]

The critics of criticism and the partisans of "everyday life" and the "commonsense world" attempt to turn democratic ideas into a defense of ignorance. If the majority of people are not interested in understanding themselves through examining their social structure and relations, they have every right to their choice. According to this reasoning, it is not significant that the expectations and rules of everyday life favor some groups at the expense of others, and that the means of disseminating information about the society are in the hands of the established and the privileged sectors. Those who fear criticism believe that expectations and rules are "socially constructed": human beings create their relations and institutions. Yet they do not acknowledge the extent to which the "social construction of reality" is achieved by those groups that have the greatest share of wealth, power, influence, and moral authority.

Behind the arguments in favor of restricting criticism, or at least of not actively encouraging it, is the judgment that while the sociologist is capable of realizing that human beings create their relations and institutions, and can change them without suffering anomie, the ordinary person has a need to believe that the relations and institutions of everyday life are necessary and just. This judgment is questionable.

First, choosing sociology (taking a sociological perspective) does not necessarily lead to anomie and, in fact, seems to work against falling into this state. The person who suffers a loss of standards, or "normlessness," is likely to be one who has lost social support rather than one who has independently undertaken self-examination. Anomie occurs when human beings are isolated from social relations and lack trust in others who might verify their opinions and judgments, when other persons who are important to them expose them to conflicting standards and demands, and when they feel that they have been rejected. The normless person may have once been a "true believer" who hung on to a shallow faith until it was destroyed by the complexities of living. Those who fall into the abyss of anomie are those who have been subjected to devastating criticism from the outside, not those who have undertaken self-criticism. The process of self-understanding has its own norms and standards that allow the person to live in critical tension and dialogue with "everyday life." Such standards as factual accuracy, precision, logical consistency, adequacy, and fruitfulness provide an alternative to belief in the necessity and goodness of current and established institutions and relations. Such methods as constructing ideal types and participant observation provide alternatives to accepting the interpretations of society and self offered in the mass media. Hence, there is nothing innate in sociologists that makes them capable of independent judgment without suffering the ravages of normlessness. Human science itself embodies norms that need not be restricted to formal inquiry but can be carried over into daily living.

Beyond the idea that criticism and anomie are two radically different states, one may doubt that it is even accurate to speak about "everyday life" or the "commonsense world" in the present era. Perhaps people shared common rules and expectations before the Protestant Reformation, which split Christianity; the Age of Exploration, which brought the West into contact with different cultures; the Industrial Revolution, which intensified occupational specialization and spawned new economic classes; and the Renaissance, which awakened Europeans to a classical, pre-Christian heritage. Since these events, some of which occurred nearly five hundred years ago, Western societies have been divided by conflicting visions of the human condition. The rules and expectations of the commonsense world have differed from one group to another, and even within what are conventionally called "groups."

As society and culture have become increasingly diversified and heterogeneous, finding unity within modern life has become a problem. In the nineteenth century most sociologists believed that diversity could be explained by some underlying principle, such as the class struggle was for Marx. For Marx, different visions of the human condition arose spontaneously from the development of fundamental class interests. In the twentieth century it has become more difficult to believe that even specialized and partial versons of everyday life arise spontaneously. Social life today is organized by vast conglomerates which attempt to define "common sense" to suit their interests in stable growth. The vision of "normal" family life presented on television shows is often less a reflection of what actually goes on within families than a manufactured standard by which families can evaluate themselves. This standard is not arbitrary, but supports consumption patterns favorable to advertisers.

Within a mass society controlled by large organizations, the choice of whether or not to take a sociological perspective is not between suffering a painful rootlessness and loss of standards, or happily performing one's appointed task within the division of labor. Rather it is a choice between becoming conscious of one's possible commitments and allowing oneself passively to accept the definitions of one's situation that have been forged by and in the interests of others. There is no absolute moral law or divine commandment that people should not accept someone else's definition of their situation. Choosing sociology is a genuine decision.

Fear of criticism and self-examination ultimately rests upon a deep pessimism about human existence. Defenders of myth and pleasing illusions need not believe that some groups are innately inferior to others; instead, they may conceive of social life as a tragedy. Perhaps it is now true that the majority of people believe that their institutions are necessary and good, and perhaps it is also true that if they suddenly lost this belief, they would either engage in a vicious struggle against one another or would wander lost and alone toward suicide. But if these hypotheses are correct, why are they so? At least in part people would be disturbed by losing their faith in the solidity of everyday life because they had never learned to trust their minds and to reach independent and informed judgments about their situations. And they had never learned to criticize because they had never been encouraged to do so within the established institutions. Hence, the institutions that perpetuate privilege are at least partly responsible for the possibility that people are not capable of changing them responsibly. There seems to be but one way of avoiding this tragedy: the expansion of genuine critical inquiry.

Types of Sociology

Choosing to take a sociological perspective involves the decision to become aware of the contexts in which one's thoughts and actions originate and for which they have consequences. Once this initial decision has been made, the person must choose how to put it into effect. This second decision is a question of choosing between different types of sociology. The preceding chapters have presented a vision of sociology as a human science based on freedom in contrast to a natural science based on determinism or, better, determination. The contrasts between sociology conceived as a human science and as a natural science are reflected in the spheres of theory, philosophy of science, method, and interpretation of action.

Liberation and Control

The central question by which different approaches to sociology can be distinguished is: What is the purpose of studying the human context? The history of social thought has shown that it is not sufficient to answer this question by stating that knowledge of the social and cultural dimensions of human existence is valuable for its own sake. Judgments about the nature of social relations (whether they are fundamentally cooperative or competitive), about the relevance of groups (whether, for example, nation or class is a more important determinant of activity), and about culture (whether human values differ greatly over time and space) not only provide interpretations about life but also affect the directions of activity. For example, someone who believes that human relations are fundamentally competitive will be less likely to make efforts to achieve cooperative networks of activity than someone who believes that cooperation is basic or who has not yet reached a decision about this issue. Hence, judgments about human social and cultural existence can be applied directly in daily life and have a practical character. Knowledge gained within the natural sciences also has effects on life through the application of technologies. But the effects are not as immediate and direct as they are in the case of judgments about the human condition, because the latter do not have to be converted into technologies before they can be applied.

Sociological knowledge has a moral dimension that is lacking in the natural sciences or in such formal disciplines as mathematics. Judgments about human relations and groups are not only accounts of what has happened, but also descriptions of the possiblities that human beings have actualized and, thus, of the possibilities that they might be capable of realizing in the future. Sociologists who believe that their science should be patterned after the natural sciences frequently claim that they are merely describing and explaining what "is." But is what has happened in the past a good indication of what people might be able to do in the future? Should the present boundaries of human achievement be made eternal limitations by sanctifying them as scientific principles? Should people attempt to strive to attain the impossible even when they believe that their efforts are doomed to failure?

These questions reveal a profound difference between a human science and a natural science. We do not think that it is a restriction when we learn that an eclipse of the moon will take place at a certain hour on a certain day one hundred years from now or that a particular comet will be visible from earth in fifty years. Yet we may feel confined and disturbed if we are told by a sociologist that there will always be dominant economic classes and ruling political elites. The difference is that we believe that we have possibilities that have not yet been actualized, whereas we do not believe that natural phenomena have such possibilities. As far as we can determine, the comet does not dream of changing its course in the way that some human beings dream of changing their social relations and structures. Whether these dreams define live options that can actually be attained or utopian fantasies, they are an integral part of human existence. Human science cannot be equated with natural science because it is at least two-dimensional. Natural scientists can confine themselves to the realm of *what has happened* or to predicting what will happen based upon past experience, while human scientists must consider *what might happen*. Imagination is an active component in human existence.

In contemporary sociology there are two major responses to the question: What is the purpose of studying the human context? One type of sociology is directed toward the goal of more effective *control* of human activity while the other has as its aim human *liberation*. Those whose implicit or explicit aim is control tend to view sociological theory as a response to the problem of order, sociology as a natural science, method as a refinement of controlled experiment, and the field of experience as restricted to publically observable behavior. Those whose goal is liberation tend to view sociological theory as a response to the problem of freedom, sociology as a human science, method as imaginative reconstruction of experience, and the field of experience as widened to include states of awareness that are not directly observable by outsiders.

The motive of control is associated with the growth of complex organizations that must engage in long-range planning to be assured of their continued functioning. Planning means that human activity must be *predictable*. A twenty-year road-building program, for example, assumes that people will still be driving automobiles in two decades. Sociologists whose work is oriented toward control are not necessarily planners themselves; but their work is structured in such a way that it is more useful to planners than to the clients, customers, and subjects of vast organizations. The attempt to discover "laws" of human behavior through the administration of questionnaires and the construction of controlled laboratory situations identifies general tendencies and regularities that allow planners to predict the consequences of organizational policies but have little or no utility for the person who does not have institutional power. For example, studies of the social characteristics of people who vote Republican may be quite useful to campaign managers who desire to spend their funds most effectively, but are at most interesting bits of information for the voter. Sociology that is directed toward control is usually confined to "movement space and time." It studies fragments of the human being, such as the linkage between voting behavior and social class. The human being is reduced to a series of points on a multitude of probability distributions, each point being a focus for a different organizational planner.

It is a short step from discovering the regularities and tendencies of mass behavior to attempting to make sure that these tendencies persist so that organizational plans will be accomplished. "Social engineering" is a relatively new field for social scientists, but it is growing rapidly as governmental agencies and business conglomerates demand studies that evaluate the success and failure of their policies and programs. Assuming that large organizations continue to dominate social life, sociologists will increasingly be called upon to advise agencies about the most effective "incentives" and "disincentives" (rewards and punishments) for realizing programs. The control orientation to sociology means that concrete human beings are treated as fragments of masses whose only role is to smile when the intervention of the planners makes them feel good and to cry out in pain when they are "inadvertently" hurt by programs.

The motive of liberation is essentially a response to a sociology oriented toward control. Those who advocate a sociology directed toward liberation acknowledge that control can be used for a broad range of goals, such as feeding, clothing, and housing the poor, and destroying towns and forests through the effective use of napalm. But they are concerned that whatever the aims of the planners may be, the one goal they cannot entertain is that human beings take charge of their own social existence and become dependent upon one another rather than upon the business, governmental, and educational conglomerates that now determine their context. If the idea of control is related to planning, the notion of liberation is bound up with self-determination. Hence, while sociologies oriented toward control begin by relating observable "behaviors" such as purchasing a product, voting, or joining an organization to "objective" factors such as sex, race, age, income, residence, or educational attainment, sociologies based on liberation begin with the process of self-understanding: *the integration by the individual of the diverse perspectives on society and culture.* Liberation-directed sociology attempts to provide people with knowledge of how organizations affect them and how they can assert themselves against control in conjunction with others. Successful resistance to power concentrations requires individuals who have sufficient trust in their informed judgment not to be frightened by claims that they are mentally ill, incompetent, or ignorant. Liberation-directed sociology cannot engineer outcomes, but it can help people gain the confidence to take greater charge of their lives.

Figure 6.1. TYPES OF SOCIOLOGY

	Liberation-Directed	*Control-Directed*
Theoretical Problem:	Problem of Freedom	Problem of Order
Type of Science:	Human Science adequacy possibility	Natural Science explanation prediction
Method:	Nonintervention by Investigator	Data Created by Investigator
Theory of Knowledge:	Expansive Empiricism	Restrictive Empiricism

FREEDOM AND ORDER

In the sphere of theory, sociologies based on liberation are distinguished from those based on control by a concern with the problem of freedom rather than the problem of order. The problem of order, which became the central focus of modern social thought in the sixteenth century, is the question of how human beings can attain sufficient unity to live with one another in a community. The first modern social thinkers, such as Machiavelli, Hobbes, and Spinoza, believed that human beings could live together without destroying one another only if there was a superior and organized force (the state) above them.[31] In the absence of such a force, people would live in mutual fear of one another, feeling that their property was perpetually in danger of being taken away from them. Succeeding thinkers in the modern age showed that other controls upon human beings prevented the "war of all against all," such as material reward, the desire for approval and praise, and feelings of moral obligation. By the turn of the twentieth century, sociologists had defined the workings of a multitude of means by which human beings keep one another under control. The human being, who for Machiavelli, Hobbes, and Spinoza was an unruly beast that had to be tamed, had become a domestic animal subject to the determination of guilt, shame, and flattery as well as coercion.

It is not difficult to understand why the early modern writers were so preoccupied with the problem of order. Religious unity, which had provided the social cement of the medieval world, was being broken at the same time that the West was coming into contact with alien cultures and its economic system was being altered. The emerging states provided a framework of power for containing the conflicts that resulted from the explosion of diversity. But in the twentieth century the terms of the problem have been completely reversed. The greatest danger to the contemporary individual is not his neighbor, but the enormous organizations that are supposed to protect and serve both of them. The concentration camps and gas chambers of the Nazis were not acts of individual greed, but state policies. The same holds for Indian reservations in the United States and labor camps in the Soviet Union. Industrial pollution that may cause cancer and other fatal diseases is not a matter of one private individual despoiling the property of another, but of organizations determining the amount of poison to which individuals will be exposed. The homeless refugees throughout the world have not been displaced by individuals or small groups trying to increase their possessions, but by organized armies directed by elites. If it is understandable why early modern thinkers looked to a limited state for protection against interindividual and intergroup conflict, it is equally understandable why some contemporary thinkers look to the liberation of individuals and communities from unlimited state and corporate domination. The problems of sociology are not beyond history. They can change as people perceive new threats and new values.

Human Science and Natural Science

Sociologists who wished to resolve the problem of order patterned the social sciences after the natural sciences, making their criteria of success the explanation and prediction of human behavior.

In accordance with these criteria they developed methods approximating controlled experiments, in which they could create the data to suit the specifications of their research. Further, they restricted themselves to studying only those phases of experience that were publically observable. Hence, there has been an analogical fit between the problem of order and the science created to solve it; paralleling the freedom/order dichotomy in theory is the freedom/determination distinction in science.

Modern sociology has been an attempt to discover the factors that narrow the wide range of possible human activities into a predictable band. This effort does not so much involve a commitment to some dogma of determinism as it implies a strategy that directs the investigator to look at what is well defined and orderly at the expense of what is ambiguous, vague, chaotic, and in the process of growth. The application of the model of natural science to sociology has produced invaluable results, particularly by uncovering the processes through which human activities are controlled. However, this model is incapable of creating a sociology that will go beyond describing how people *have been* dominated and how they *have* controlled one another in the past. A human science based on freedom rather than determination does not seek to predict human activity, but to define the alternative possibilities for social relations and to relate them to present situations. Such a human science is no more committed to a dogma of free will than the natural science model is committed to absolute determinism. It does imply a strategy that directs the investigator to look for those events and processes that seem to run counter to the established order and that may generate issues around which people can mobilize to gain greater self-determination. Most of the inquiry demanded by a human science can be carried out by individuals who have initiated the process of self-understanding and who are willing to consider the events of their daily lives from several perspectives, draw parallels between their experiences (construct ideal types), and observe their dealings with others with some detachment from immediate interest.

EXERCISE

Do you think that contemporary society would undergo many changes if a majority of people took a sociological perspective rather than one suppled by "common sense," advertising, or propaganda?

What kinds of changes would occur, if any? Can people successfully change their perspective without changing the institutions in which they live? Do changes in perspective lead to changes in institutions or is the reverse the case?

EXERCISE

Criticize liberation-directed sociology from the viewpoint of control-directed sociology.

CONCLUSION

Sociology cannot be separated from personal life because it is knowledge about that life. Those who study sociology and come away indifferent to it and unaffected by it have *chosen* to ignore its insights and not to take it seriously. There is nothing magical about knowledge. It is always possible to learn about something and then to say: "So what!" Contrary to Socrates and other optimists throughout Western history, knowledge does not necessarily lead to virtue. Knowledge in the natural sciences can be used to preserve life or to destroy it. Knowledge in the human sciences can be used to expand awareness and possibilities, or it can be employed to dominate and manipulate others, or it can simply be ignored.

As Dostoevsky pointed out over and over again, people can go against the dictates of their own interest or of their conscience out of simple spite or just to prove that they are free. One of the paradoxes of human science is that the rational process of self-understanding discloses the capacity for human beings to act irrationally. Perhaps the basic point of our discussion in this book has been that the self is a process of freedom rather than an object or "property." Yet most people seem to think of themselves and others as objects that can be frozen into images just as faces are frozen in photographs. Obviously it is possible for people to choose not to be free! Freedom is, after all, one value among many; and it may not even usually be consistent with happiness or pleasure. Taking a sociological perspective involves the rejection of viewing oneself as an isolated and independent individual. This commitment requires conscious choice. Once one has decided to take a sociological perspective, one must determine the kind of sociology to pursue. Again the commitment demands choice.

Sociology as a Commitment

We have attempted to present the case for taking a sociological perspective and for treating sociology as a human science rather than as a natural science. We are aware of the barriers to self-understanding because we have faced them and surmounted some of them, at least to a limited extent. We invite others to join us, but we do not promise pleasure and contentment. Broadened awareness means more conflicting experience to integrate and more options to consider. Sociology as a human science is a preparation for freedom. But freedom itself must be chosen.

NOTES

Chapter 1. THE HUMAN CONDITION

1. Bertrand Russell, *Has Man a Future?* (Baltimore: Penguin Books, 1961), p. 127.

2. Jean-Paul Sartre, *Being and Nothingness* (New York: Philosophical Library, 1956); Sartre, *Nausea* (New York: New Directions, 1964).

3. E. H. Carr, *The New Society* (New York: St. Martin's Press, 1960).

4. Joe McGinniss, *The Selling of the President, 1968* (New York: Trident Press, 1969).

5. The relations between social science and despair are discussed by theorists of mass society. See William Barrett, *What is Existentialism?* (New York: Grove Press, 1964); E. H. Carr, *What is History?* (New York: Knopf, 1961); José Ortega y Gasset, *The Revolt of the Masses* (New York: New American Library, 1950); Karl Jaspers, *Man in the Modern Age* (Garden City, N.Y.: Doubleday, n.d.).

6. Talcott Parsons has described this "deflationary cycle" in social relations. See Talcott Parsons, *Politics and Social Structure* (New York: Free Press, 1969).

7. Henry W. Malcolm, "The Crisis in Morality: Human vs. Institutional," *New University Thought* 5 (Special Issue, 1966–67): 92.

8. Bertrand Russell has distinguished between knowledge by acquaintance and knowledge by description. See Bertrand Russell, *The Problems of Philosophy* (London: Oxford University Press, 1957), pp. 46–59.

9. The belief that money is the most important factor in human existence is reflected in the best seller list. For example, see Adam Smith, *The Money Game* (New York: Random House, 1968).

10. David Riesman with Nathan Glazer and Reuel Denney, *The Lonely Crowd* (New Haven: Yale University Press, 1961). For experiments on conformity see Solomon E. Asch, "Effects of Group Pressure upon the Modification and Distortion of Judgments," in *Groups, Leadership and Men*, ed. H. Guetzkow (Pittsburgh: Carnegie Press, 1951), pp. 177–90.

11. The idea that there are elites of wealth and power in contemporary societies is long-standing, but not undisputed, in sociology. The history of this view can be found in James H. Meisel, *The Myth of the Ruling Class* (Ann Arbor: University of Michigan Press, 1962); Renzo Sereno, *The Rulers* (New York: Frederick A. Praeger, 1962).

12. R. D. Laing, *The Politics of Experience* (New York: Ballantine Books, 1967); Philip Rieff, *The Triumph of the Therapeutic* (New York: Harper & Row, 1966).

13. This attitude has been called "vulgar pragmatism." See Abraham Kaplan, *American Ethics and Public Policy* (New York: Oxford University Press, 1963).

14. Howard Ross Smith, *Democracy and the Public Interest* (Athens: University of Georgia Press, 1960).

15. Elijah Jordan described this phenomenon as the "sale situation." See his *Business be Damned* (New York: H. Schuman, 1952).

16. McGinniss, *The Selling of the President*.

17. The unity of thought and action is a central principle of many schools of twentieth-century thought, for example, Marxism, pragmatism, and existential phenomenology. See Joan Huber Rytina and Charles P. Loomis, "Marxist Dialectic and Pragmatism: Power as Knowledge," *American Sociological Review* 35 (April 1970): 308–18.

18. Jules Henry has described the implicit philosophy of advertising. See his *Culture Against Man* (New York: Random House, 1963).

19. Riesman et al., *The Lonely Crowd*; Jay M. Jackson and Herbert D. Saltzstein, "The Effect of Person-Group Relationships on Conformity Processes," *Journal of Abnormal and Social Psychology* 57 (1958): 17–24.

20. McGinniss, *The Selling of the President*.

21. The judgment that basic beliefs about the human condition affect others besides the individual people who hold them is rooted in an existentialist perspective on the human condition. See Michael A. and Deena Weinstein, "Sartre and the Humanist Tradition in Sociology," in *Sartre: A Collection of Critical Essays*, ed. Mary Warnock (Garden City, N.Y.: Doubleday, 1971), pp. 357–86.

22. Georges Sorel, *Reflections on Violence* (Glencoe, Ill.: Free Press, 1950); Seymour M. Lipset, *Political Man* (Garden City, N.Y.: Doubleday, 1963).

23. Some social thinkers believe that personal growth is a middle-class luxury or illusion. See Frantz Fanon, *The Wretched of the Earth* (New York: Grove Press, 1965); Michael Novak, "Politicizing the Lower Middle," *Commonweal* 40 (6 June 1969): 343.

24. Regis Debray, *Revolution in the Revolution?* (New York: Monthly Review Press, 1967).
25. Arthur Bentley developed the concept of "clotting." See his *Relativity in Man and Society* (New York: G. P. Putnam's Sons, 1926).
26. The origins of the idea that the self is property have been discussed by C. B. Macpherson in his *The Political Theory of Possessive Individualism* (Oxford: Clarendon Press, 1962).
27. Sigmund Freud, *A General Introduction to Psychoanalysis* (Garden City, N.Y.: Doubleday, 1953); Abraham H. Maslow, *Motivation and Personality* (New York: Harper & Row, 1954).
28. Augustine, *The City of God* (New York: Hafner, 1948), IV: 4.
29. Michael A. Weinstein, "New Ways and Old to Talk About Politics," *Review of Politics* 35 (January 1973): 41–60.
30. The social relativity of the idea that human beings are inherently greedy is shown by E. T. Hiller, *The Nature and Basis of Social Order* (New Haven: College and University Press, 1966); Radhakamal Mukerjee, *The Philosophy of Social Science* (London: Macmillan, 1960).
31. William H. Whyte, Jr., *The Organization Man* (Garden City, N.Y.: Doubleday, 1957).
32. John Kenneth Galbraith has presented a defense of committees in his *The New Industrial State* (Boston: Houghton Mifflin, 1971).
33. Whyte, *The Organization Man.*
34. C. Wright Mills, *The Sociological Imagination* (New York: Grove Press, 1958).
35. Uniqueness of the self is a prominent theme in American thought. See Josiah Royce, *The World and the Individual,* vol. 2 (New York: Dover Books, 1959).
36. The defense of tradition has been undertaken by many twentieth-century conservatives. See Russell Kirk, *The Conservative Mind* (Chicago: Henry Regnery, 1954); Robert A. Nisbet, *Community and Power* (New York: Oxford University Press, 1962).
37. Ortega y Gasset, *The Revolt of the Masses.*
38. The systematic analysis of world-views and their social relativity has been undertaken by F. S. C. Northrop, *The Meeting of East and West* (New York: Macmillan, 1946); Stephen C. Pepper, *World Hypotheses* (Los Angeles: University of California Press, 1957); Pitirim Sorokin, *Sociological Theories of Today* (New York: Harper & Row, 1966).
39. The analysis of the relations between beliefs about the human condition and social groupings is called the sociology of knowledge. See Peter L. Berger and Thomas Luckmann, *The Social Construction of Reality* (Garden City, N.Y.: Doubleday, 1966); Burkart Holzner, *Reality Construction in Society* (Cambridge, Mass.: Schenckman, 1968); Karl Mannheim, *Essays on the Sociology of Knowledge* (London: Routledge & Kegan Paul, 1952); Robert K. Merton, *Social Theory and Social Structure* (Glencoe, Ill.: Free Press, 1949).
40. Karl Marx and Friedrich Engels, *The Communist Manifesto* (New York: Appleton-Century-Crofts, 1955), pp. 29–30.
41. This situation has been called mental "entropy" by Gunter Remmling. See his *Road to Suspicion* (New York: Appleton-Century-Crofts, 1967).
42. Gyorgy Lukacs, *History and Class Consciousness* (Cambridge, Mass.: MIT Press 1971).

43. For a critique of this view, see Robert Boguslaw, *The New Utopians* (Englewood Cliffs, N.J.: Prentice-Hall, 1963).

44. This phenomenon has been referred to as "pseudo-gemeinschaft" by Fritz Pappenheim. See his *The Alienation of Modern Man* (New York: Monthly Review Press, 1959), p. 68.

45. Stokely Carmichael and Charles V. Hamilton, *Black Power* (New York: Random House, 1967); Eldridge Cleaver, *Soul on Ice* (New York: McGraw-Hill, 1968).

46. R. D. Laing, *Self and Others* (New York: Pantheon Books, 1969).

47. W. I. Thomas identified the "self-fulfilling prophecy." See his *On Social Organization and Social Personality* (Chicago: University of Chicago Press, 1966).

48. The idea that the human condition is trivial may be referred to as "vulgar existentialism," similar to Kaplan's "vulgar pragmatism." For a serious interpretation of the "absurd," see Albert Camus, *The Myth of Sisyphus and Other Essays* (New York: Knopf, 1955).

49. Such indecision when confronted with multiple possibilities is another vulgarization of contemporary philosophy. In this case, the philosophical school of phenomenology uses the bracketing of commitment to aid in the analysis of conscious experience, not to hinder action. Human beings cannot live in the "realm of essence" though they may experience multiple perspectives.

50. Justus Buchler has referred to the "spoliation of the possible" involved in any human action. See his *Toward a General Theory of Human Judgment* (New York: Columbia University Press, 1951).

Chapter 2. A BRIEF GUIDE TO SOCIAL THOUGHT

1. For some "maps" of social thought, see Don Martindale, *The Nature and Types of Sociological Theory* (Boston: Houghton Mifflin, 1960); Nicholas S. Timasheff, *Sociological Theory* (New York: Random House, 1957).

2. The idea was suggested in a personal letter to one of the authors from Professor Haring, dated January 24, 1971.

3. Peter M. Blau, *Exchange and Power in Social Life* (New York: Wiley, 1967).

4. John Courtney Murray, *We Hold These Truths* (Garden City, N.J.: Doubleday, 1964), p. 310.

5. Ibid.

6. Ibid., p. 311.

7. Ibid.

8. Sidney Hook, *Political Power and Personal Freedom* (New York: Collier Books, 1962), p. 73.

9. Erich Fromm, "Man for Himself," in *Philosophy for a Time of Crisis*, ed. Adrienne Koch (New York: E. P. Dutton, 1959), pp. 166–67.

10. Mary Elizabeth Walsh and Paul Hanly Furfey, *Social Problems and Social Action* (Englewood Cliffs, N.J.: Prentice-Hall, 1958), p. 4.

11. Ibid., p. 11.

12. Ibid., p. 4.

13. Karl Marx and Friedrich Engels, *The Communist Manifesto* (New York: Appleton-Century-Crofts, Inc., 1955), p. 9.

14. Ibid., p. 22.
15. Ibid., p. 27.
16. Ibid., p. 28.
17. Simone de Beauvoir, *The Second Sex* (New York: Knopf, 1952); Kate Millett, *Sexual Politics* (New York: Avon, 1970).
18. See Talcott Parsons' *Social System* (Glencoe, Ill.: Free Press, 1951) for such a division into sectors.
19. Talcott Parsons, *The Structure of Social Action* (Glencoe, Ill.: Free Press, 1949).
20. Herbert Marcuse, *Reason and Revolution* (Boston: Beacon Press, 1960), p. vii.
21. See the list of suggested readings at the end of this chapter for some major works of these schools of thought.
22. George Santayana, *Dominations and Powers* (New York: Charles Scribner's Sons, 1953). See the excellent discussion of liberty in the first several chapters.

Chapter 3. SOCIOLOGY AND SCIENCE

1. The view of human science presented in this chapter is not the only one. Many sociologists believe that the human sciences should follow the model of the natural sciences and seek to explain social activity in terms of invariant or statistical relations between events. Our viewpoint is that human science should describe intentions, purposes, and analogies, as well as finding correlations and causal laws.
2. Science fiction has relied heavily on this interpretation. See Karel Capek, *R.U.R.* (Garden City, N.Y.: Doubleday, 1923); Capek, *War With the Newts* (New York: G. P. Putnam's Sons, 1937); Mary Shelley, *Frankenstein* (New York: Dutton, 1963).
3. The legal theorist Jerome Frank presented the grounds for "fact skepticism" in the legal process. See his *Courts on Trial* (Princeton: Princeton University Press, 1949). See also Wilfrid E. Rumble, *American Legal Realism* (Ithaca: Cornell University Press, 1968).
4. An extended discussion of the ways in which facts are relative to images of the human context is found in Pitirim Sorokin, *Social and Cultural Dynamics*, 4 vols. (New York: American Book, 1937–41).
5. Robin George Collingwood, *The Idea of History* (Oxford: Clarendon Press, 1946).
6. Thomas S. Kuhn, *The Structure of Scientific Revolutions* (Chicago: University of Chicago Press, 1962).
7. Example of this perspective are Floyd Hunter, *Community Power Structure* (Chapel Hill: University of North Carolina Press, 1968); C. Wright Mills, *The Power Elite* (New York: Oxford University Press, 1956).
8. An example of this perspective is David Easton, *A Systems Analysis of Political Life* (New York: Wiley, 1965).
9. This perspective is developed by Jean-Paul Sartre in his *Search for a Method* (New York: Random House, 1968).
10. Alvin W. Gouldner, *The Coming Crisis of Western Sociology* (New York: Basic Books, 1970).
11. Sartre, *Search for a Method*.

12. This is the way in which William James saw original experience.
13. George Herbert Mead, *Mind, Self and Society* (Chicago: University of Chicago Press, 1947).
14. Gordon W. Allport, *The Nature of Prejudice* (Garden City, N.Y.: Doubleday, 1958).
15. This attitude, which is quite popular, was expressed in the eighteenth century by Edmund Burke in his *Reflections on the Revolution in France* (London: Dent, 1960).
16. This question is phrased in terms of "applied science"—What is the most effective way of realizing a goal? A similar question can be asked from a pure science perspective—What are the effects of an institution on other social relations? For example—Do day-care centers weaken family ties?
17. All public issues are debated within wider frameworks about the nature of human affairs. For example, the "energy crisis" and "environmental pollution" carry judgments about the actual and possible relations of human beings to nature.
18. Susanne Langer, *Philosophy in a New Key* (New York: New American Library, 1964).
19. This procedure is called "operationalization"—the effort to define terms by repeatable physical operations. See Abraham Kaplan, *The Conduct of Inquiry* (San Francisco: Chandler, 1964), pp. 39–42.
20. Henry Pratt Fairchild, ed., *Dictionary of Sociology* (Ames: Littlefield, Adams & Co., 1955), p. 336.
21. The idea that the process of naming is itself creative of human experience and meaning is emphasized by John Dewey and Arthur F. Bentley in their *Knowing and the Known* (Boston: Beacon Press, 1949).
22. The ways in which definitions of violence can be shifted can be grasped by considering two contrasting discussions of the terms. See Newton Garver, "What Violence Is," *Nation* 206 (24 June 1968): 820; Robert E. Fitch, "The Uses of Violence," *Christian Century* 85 (17 April 1968): 483.
23. The uses of "word magic" are catalogued and analyzed in the discipline of general semantics. See Alfred Korzybski, *Science and Sanity* (New York: International Non-Aristotelian Library Publishing, 1941); S. I. Hayakawa, *Language in Thought and Action* (New York: Harcourt Brace Jovanovich, 1972).
24. For the corruption of language and its possible consequences, see George Orwell, *1984* (New York: New American Library, 1961).
25. Arnold Rose has emphasized the importance of contradiction in revealing "covert culture"—the judgments underlying rhetoric. See his "Varieties of Sociological Imagination," *American Sociological Review* 34 (October 1969): 625.
26. On middle-class snobbery, see Andrew M. Greeley, *Why Can't They Be Like Us?* (New York: Dutton, 1971).
27. For proponents of the natural science view, see George C. Homans, *The Nature of Social Science* (New York: Harcourt Brace Jovanovich, 1967); Hans L. Zetterberg, *On Theory and Verification in Sociology* (Totowa: Bedminster Press, 1965).
28. John Stuart Mill, *Utilitarianism* (Indianapolis: Bobbs-Merrill, 1971).
29. The notion that insight is the final test of judgments about the human condition appears in the works of many twentieth-century sociologists. Georges Gurvitch speaks of "direct integration into wholes in *Traité de Sociologie*

(Paris: Presses Universitaires de France, 1958–60). Similarly, Paul Hanly Furfey discusses an "integrative sociology" based on insight in *The Scope and Method of Sociology* (New York: Harper, 1953).

30. The extension of self-understanding is one of the goals of our public morality. For a similar statement, see Thomas Landon Thorson, *The Logic of Democracy* (New York: Holt, Rinehart & Winston, 1962).

31. The social movement Technocracy bases its propaganda on the theme that people do not have a choice about whether or not government by experts will come about, but that they do have a chance to aid in the arrival of such a government. People, thus, have a chance not a choice.

Chapter 4. METHOD WITHOUT MADNESS

1. William Ernest Hocking, "Marcel and the Ground Issues of Metaphysics," *Philosophy and Phenomenological Research* 14 (June 1954): 465.

2. Abraham Kaplan, *The Conduct of Inquiry* (San Francisco: Chandler, 1964), p. 28.

3. Alfred de Grazia, ed., *The Velikovsky Affair* (New Hyde Park, N.Y.: University Books, 1966).

4. Thomas S. Kuhn, *The Structure of Scientific Revolutions* (Chicago: University of Chicago Press, 1962).

5. For some of the debates which have characterized the history of sociology, see Roscoe C. and Gisela J. Hinkle, *The Development of Modern Sociology* (Garden City, N.Y.: Doubleday, 1954).

6. George A. Lundberg, *Can Science Save Us?* (New York: David McKay, 1961.

7. Richard LaPiere, "Attitudes vs. Actions," *Social Forces* 13 (March 1934): 230-7.

8. Eugene J. Webb et al., *Unobtrusive Measures: Nonreactive Research in the Social Sciences* (Chicago: Rand McNally, 1966).

9. A related phenomenon, in which people change their behavior simply because they know that they are being studied, is called the "Hawthorn effect." See Leon Festinger and Daniel Katz, *Research Methods in the Behavioral Sciences* (New York: Holt, Rinehart & Winston, 1953), p. 101.

10. Don D. Smith, "Levels of Political Information in the American Public" (Paper presented at the annual meetings of the Southern Sociological Society, Atlanta, Georgia, 1968).

11. Floyd Hunter, *Community Power Structure* (Chapel Hill: University of North Carolina Press, 1953).

12. E. H. Carr, *The New Society* (New York: St. Martin's Press, 1960), p. 13.

13. Durkheim used many other methods besides the historical method. For example, he used the demographic method in his study of suicide.

14. For examples of ideal types, see Hans Gerth and C. Wright Mills, eds., *From Max Weber* (New York: Oxford University Press, 1946).

15. Hannah Arendt, *The Origins of Totalitarianism* (New York: Meridian Books, 1958).

16. Ferdinand Toennies, *Community and Society* (East Lansing: Michigan State University Press, 1957).

17. Emile Durkheim, *The Division of Labor in Society* (Glencoe, Ill.: Free Press, 1947).

18. Emile Durkheim, *Suicide* (Glencoe, Ill.: Free Press, 1951).

19. For a discussion of the various explanations of political violence, see H. L. Nieburg, *Political Violence* (New York: St. Martin's Press, 1969).

20. Erving Goffman, *Asylums* (Garden City, N.Y.: Doubleday, 1961).

21. Elliot Liebow, *Tally's Corner* (Boston: Little, Brown, 1967).

22. Webb et al., *Unobtrusive Measures.* See particularly the section "Contrived Observation: Hidden Hardware and Control," pp. 142–70.

23. Bronislaw Malinowski, *Argonauts of the Western Pacific* (New York: Dutton, 1961), p. 18. Malinowski developed the technique of participant observation.

24. For example, see William F. Whyte, *Street Corner Society: The Social Structure of an Italian Slum* (Chicago: University of Chicago Press, 1955).

25. For examples of nonparticipant observation, see Peter M. Blau, *The Dynamics of Bureaucracy* (Chicago: University of Chicago Press, 1963).

26. See the special issue "On Language and Conduct," *Sociological Focus* 3 (Winter 1969–70), particularly the articles by Irwin Deutscher, Aaron V. Cicourel, and R. Bruce Anderson.

27. Martin Trow, "Small Businessmen, Political Tolerance and Support for McCarthy," *American Journal of Sociology* 64 (1958): 270–81.

28. Pitirim Sorokin, *Fads and Foibles in Modern Sociology and Related Sciences* (Chicago: Henry Regnery, 1956).

29. Stanley Milgram, "Behavioral Study of Obedience," *Journal of Abnormal and Social Psychology* 67 (1963): 371–78.

30. Harold Leavitt, "Some Effects of Certain Communication Patterns on Group Performance," *Journal of Abnormal and Social Psychology* 46 (1951): 38–50.

31. Fritz J. Roethlisberger and William J. Dickson, *Management and the Worker* (Cambridge, Mass.: Harvard University Press, 1943).

32. Harold Guetzkow, ed., *Simulation in Social Science* (Englewood Cliffs, N.J.: Prentice-Hall, 1962).

Chapter 5. HUMAN ACTION

1. Restrictive empiricism began with the eighteenth-century Scottish philosopher David Hume who rejected the idea that people could be intuitive about self-evident truths. For Hume, what is known is what is sensed. In the nineteenth century Auguste Comte argued that science could only be based on associations between observed events, not on "causes" (which could not be sensed). In the twentieth century logical positivists and behaviorists have carried on the tradition of restrictive empiricism, altering it to include standards of logical consistency which are not sensed.

2. The idea that only "publicly observable" experiences are open to scientific investigation has been held by many social thinkers. Logical positivists speak of verifying hypotheses through sense experience ("the verification principle"). Pragmatists speak of reducing concepts to physical operations ("operationalization"). Some phenomenologists speak of socially constructed shared experience as the basis of science ("intersubjectivity").

3. Recently, a new discipline, "the sociology of sociology," has grown up to study the social context of sociological research. See Larry T. Reynolds and Janice M. Reynolds, eds., *The Sociology of Sociology* (New York: David McKay, 1970).

4. The revolt against restrictive empiricism began at the turn of the twentieth century when William James coined the term "radical empiricism" to name the critical description of all human experience. At the same time the European movement of "phenomenology" led by Edmund Husserl widened the definition of experience in a way similar to James. Sociologists who have adopted an expansive definition of experience to guide their work include Georges Gurvitch ("hyper-empiricism"), Maurice Hauriou ("hyper-positivism") and Pitirim Sorokin ("integral epistemology").

5. Michael A. Weinstein, "New Ways and Old to Talk About Politics," *Review of Politics* 35 (January 1973): 41–60.

6. Joseph Kockelmans, ed., *Phenomenology* (Garden City, N.Y.: Doubleday, 1967). See especially part 3, "Phenomenology and the Sciences of Man," pp. 411–555.

7. David Easton, *The Political System* (New York: Alfred A. Knopf, 1953).

8. Georges Gurvitch, *Dialectique et Sociologie* (Paris: Flammarion, 1962), 8. Translation was done by the authors.

9. Ibid., p. 7.

10. The dialogic view of the self is taken by "symbolic interactionists" in sociology. See Jerome G. Manis and Bernard N. Meltzer, eds., *Symbolic Interaction* (Boston: Allyn & Bacon, 1967).

11. Henri Bergson made the intuition of time the basis of his philosophy. See his *Creative Evolution* (New York: Modern Library, 1944).

12. For the changing notions of the proper scope of sociology, see Don Martindale, *The Nature and Types of Sociological Theory* (Boston: Houghton Mifflin, 1960).

13. Auguste Comte held the view that sociology was the master science.

14. Among others, the British sociologist Morris Ginsberg held that sociologists should investigate the relations among different areas of human existence.

15. The view that sociology takes what is left after the other social sciences have made their choices of subject matter is sometimes called the garbage-can theory.

16. The problem-solving or pragmatic view of sociology is exemplified in John Dewey's *The Public and its Problems* (New York: Henry Holt, 1927).

17. Martindale, *The Nature and Types of Sociological Theory*.

18. Ibid., pp. 17–19.

19. Ernst Cassirer, *An Essay on Man* (New Haven: Yale University Press, 1944).

20. Peter L. Berger and Thomas Luckmann, *The Social Construction of Reality* (Garden City, N.Y.: Doubleday, 1966).

21. The belief that one's culture puts one at the center of human affairs is called "ethnocentrism." See William Graham Sumner, *Folkways* (New York: New American Library, 1960), pp. 27–30. "Ethnocentrism is the technical name for this view of things in which one's own group is the center of everything and all others are scaled and rated with reference to it" (pp. 27–28).

22. Discussions of individualism are found in: John Dewey, *Individualism Old and New* (New York: G. P. Putnam's Sons, 1962); William Ernest Hocking, *The Lasting Elements of Individualism* (New Haven: Yale University Press, 1937); David L. Miller, *Individualism* (Austin: University of Texas Press, 1967); David Riesman, *Individualism Reconsidered* (Glencoe, Ill.: Free Press, 1954).

23. Arthur F. Bentley, *Behavior, Knowledge, Fact* (Bloomington, Ind.: Principia Press, 1935). We thank Dr. Randall E. Triplett for sharing with us the results of his analysis of Bentley's treatment of the category of space in social science.

24. Kurt Lewin, *Field Theory and Social Science* (New York: Harper, 1951).

25. A.L. Kroeber, *Anthropology* (New York: Harcourt Brace Jovanovich, 1963). Kroeber coined the term "superorganic" to refer to culture.

26. This position is "phenomenological" in that intention is made an integral part of the action to be described. The opposing position, "behaviorism," studies only public observable "behavior," leaving intention out of its accounts of action.

27. MacQuilkin De Grange, *The Nature and Elements of Sociology* (New Haven: Yale University Press, 1953).

28. The use of social and biographical "background data" in survey research illustrates the importance of action-time to sociologists.

29. An overview of the humanistic movement in sociology can be found in John F. Glass and John R. Staude, eds., *Humanistic Society* (Pacific Palisades, Calif.: Goodyear Publishing, 1972).

30. The notion of the self as an achievement is developed by Justus Buchler in his *Toward a General Theory of Human Judgment* (New York: Columbia University Press, 1951).

31. Florian Znaniecki, *The Cultural Sciences: Their Origin and Development* (Urbana: University of Illinois Press, 1952), p. 212.

Chapter 6. SOCIOLOGY AS A COMMITMENT

1. Alvin W. Gouldner, *The Coming Crisis of Western Sociology* (New York: Basic Books, 1970), p. 490.

2. Ibid.

3. Ibid., p. 493.

4. See chapter 2 for a discussion of the relations between process theory and the natural law, monist, and pluralist alternatives.

5. See Dusky Lee Smith, "Sociology and the Rise of Corporate Capitalism," *Science and Society* 29 (Fall 1965): 1–18; Herman and Julia Geshwender, *Sociologists of the Chair* (New York: Basic Books, 1975).

6. Clark Kerr, "Selections from 'The Uses of the University,' " in *The Berkeley Student Revolt: Facts and Interpretations*, ed. Seymour Martin Lipset and Sheldon S. Wolin (Garden City, N.Y.: Doubleday, 1965).

7. Robin M. Williams, Jr., *American Society* (New York: Knopf, 1960), pp. 318–19.

8. Richard Fallenbaum, "University Abdicates Social Responsibility," in Lipset and Wolin, *The Berkeley Student Revolt*, p. 64.

9. Kenneth D. Roose and Charles J. Anderson, *A Rating of Graduate Programs* (Washington, D.C.: American Council on Education, 1970), pp. 5–8.

10. Bradford Cleaveland, "A Letter to Undergraduates," in Lipset and Wolin, *The Berkeley Student Revolt*, p. 49.

11. James Ridgeway, *The Closed Corporation* (New York: Random House, 1968).

12. Kerr, "Selections from 'The Uses of the University,' " p. 49.

13. Robert H. Connery, ed., "The Corporation and the Campus," *Proceedings of the Academy of Political Science* 30 (1970): 92. Student tuition and fees account for 18% of the university's income, federal government support 24%, state and local government support 25%, private gifts and grants 8%, income from auxiliary enterprises 12%, other income (e.g., loans 11%, and endowment earnings 2%.)

14. See Weber's essay "Science as a Vocation," in *From Max Weber,* ed. Hans Gerth and C. Wright Mills (New York: Oxford University Press, 1946).

15. Alvin W. Gouldner, "Anti-Minotaur: The Myth of a Value Free Sociology," *Social Problems* 9 (Winter 1962): 199–213.

16. Thomas S. Kuhn, *The Structure of Scientific Revolutions* (Chicago: University of Chicago Press, 1962), p. x.

17. For an extended discussion of the issue of research problem selection, see Deena Weinstein, "Bases for Choosing Research," (Paper presented at the annual meetings of the Midwest Sociological Society, Chicago, Illinois, 1975).

18. Melvin L. De Fleur, *Theories of Mass Communication* (New York: David McKay, 1970), p. 165.

19. Ibid., p. 167.

20. Ibid.

21. Ibid.

22. Gustave LeBon, *The Crowd* (New York: Viking, 1960), p. 37.

23. Ibid.

24. Leon Festinger, *A Theory of Cognitive Dissonance* (New York: Harper & Row, 1957).

25. Ibid.

26. Leon Festinger and J. Merrill Carlsmith, "Cognitive Consequences of Forced Compliance," *Journal of Abnormal and Social Psychology* 58 (1959): 203–10.

27. "Anomie" was described by Emile Durkheim in his *Suicide: A Study of Sociology* (New York: Free Press, 1951).

28. W. H. D. Rouse, trans., *Great Dialogues of Plato* (New York: New American Library, 1956).

29. Edmund Burke, *Reflections on the Revolution in France* (London: Dent, 1960).

30. This view of everyday life and critical reflection appears in Peter L. Berger and Thomas Luckmann, *The Social Construction of Reality* (Garden City, N.Y.: Doubleday, 1966); Burkart Holzner, *Reality Construction in Society* (Cambridge, Mass.: Schenkman, 1968).

31. See Niccolo Machiavelli, *The Prince* (New York: New American Library, 1952); Thomas Hobbes, *Leviathan,* parts 1 and 2 (Indianapolis: Bobbs-Merrill, 1958); Benedict de Spinoza, *A Theologico-Political Treatise and Political Treatise* (New York: Dover Publications, 1955).

Index

Accuracy, factual, 62–69
Action, human, 47, 52, 81–82, 129
　creative, 140
　full, 129, 140
　habitual, 140
　reproductive, 140
Advertising, 9, 53, 66, 68–69, 104, 148–50, 154–55
Allport, Gordon W., 175n.
Anderson, Charles J., 179n.
Anderson, R. Bruce, 177n.
Anomie, 158, 156–60
Arendt, Hannah, 176n.
Asch, Solomon E., 171n.
Association, method of. *See* Behaviorism
Augustine, 172n.

Barnum, P. T., 12
Barrett, William, 170n.
Becker, Howard S., 115, 116
Behaviorism, 153–55, 156
Belongingness, 19–20, 23–25
Bentley, Arthur F., 48, 58, 133, 134, 135, 137, 172n., 175n., 179n.
Berger, Peter L., 4, 172n., 178n., 180n.
Bergson, Henri, 122, 178n.
Blau, Peter M., 58, 113–14, 173n., 177n.
Boguslaw, Robert, 173n.
Bosserman, Philip, 59
Bourgeoisie, 43–44, 148
Buchler, Justus, 173n., 179n.
Burke, Edmund, 158, 175n., 180n.

Camus, Albert, 173n.
Capek, Karel, 174n.
Carlsmith, J. Merrill, 180n.
Carmichael, Stokely, 173n.
Carr, E. H., 92, 170n., 176n.
Case-study method. *See* Social research, methods of
Cassirer, Ernst, 178n.
Causation, 41
Chamberlain, Houston S., 56
Childe, V. Gordon, 56
Cicourel, Aaron V., 177n.
Clarification, 7–16, 99
　class struggle, 148
　Marxist interpretation, 42–43
Cleaveland, Bradford, 179n.
Cleaver, Eldridge, 173n.
Cognitive dissonance, 155–56
Coleman, James S., 110
Collingwood, R. G., 174n.
Commitment, 28–32, 108, 156
Communist Manifesto, 42–44, 56
Comte, Auguste, 94, 177n., 178n.
Connery, Robert H., 180n.
Consistency, logical, 73–75
Cooley, Charles H., 122
Crowds, 151–53
Cultural object, 125, 130–31, 136

Dahrendorf, Ralf, 57
de Beauvior, Simone, 174n.

Debray, Regis, 172n.
De Fleur, Melvin L., 149, 150, 180n.
DeGrange, MacQuilkin, 57, 179n.
de Grazia, Alfred, 176n.
Denney, Reuel, 171n.
Depersonification, 17–20
Depth-interview method. *See* Social research, methods of
Determinism, 78
Deutscher, Irwin, 177n.
Dewey, John, 175n., 178n.
Dickson, William J., 177n.
Dostoevsky, Feodor, 168
Durkheim, Emile, 48, 57, 93, 94, 96–98, 111, 112, 176n., 177n., 180n.

Easton, David, 174n., 178n.
Elites, 9, 27, 110–11
Empiricism
　expansive, 121–25
　restrictive, 119–21
Engels, Friedrich, 42, 56, 172n., 173n.
"Everyday life," 157–59
Existentialism, 52
Experience, 52, 122–23
　creative, 124–25
　cultural, 124
　lived, 123–24
　social, 124
Experimental method. *See* Social research, methods of

Fairchild, Henry P., 175n.
Fallenbaum, Richard, 144, 179n.
Fanon, Frantz, 171n.
Festinger, Leon, 176n., 180n.
Fitch, Robert E., 175n.
Frank, Jerome, 174n.
Freedom, 45–46, 52–53, 64–65, 78, 163, 165, 167–69
Freud, Sigmund, 40, 55, 172n.
Freudianism, 35
Furfey, Paul Hanly, 39, 40, 55, 173n., 176n.

Galbraith, John Kenneth, 172n.
Games, as an image of life, 108
Garver, Newton, 175n.
Generalization, 16–23, 104
Gerth, H. H., 58, 179n.
Geshwender, Herman, 143, 179n.
Geshwender, Julia, 143, 179n.
Ginsberg, Morris, 4, 178n.
Glass, John F., 179n.
Glazer, Nathan, 171n.
Goebbels, Joseph, 12
Goffman, Erving, 4, 58, 112, 113, 177n.
Gouldner, Alvin W., 142, 174n., 179n., 180n.
Greeley, Andrew, 175n.
Groups, 48, 100–101, 129
　small, 107–8
Gurvitch, Georges, 4, 59, 122, 123, 125, 137, 175n., 178n.

Hamilton, Charles V., 173n.
Haring, Phillip S. J., 34, 173n.
Hauriou, Maurice, 122, 178n.
Hayakawa, S. I., 175n.
Henry, Jules, 171n.
Hiller, E. T., 4, 59, 172n.
Hinkle, Gisela J., 176n.
Hinkle, Roscoe C., 176n.
Historical method. *See* Social research, methods of
Hobbes, Thomas, 165–66, 180n.
Hocking, William Ernest, 4, 86, 176n., 178n.
Holzner, Burkart, 172n., 180n.
Homans, George C., 175n.
Hook, Sidney, 38, 173n.
Human condition, visions of, 8, 34–36, 55–59, 61, 64–65, 79–80, 85–86, 89, 94
　compared to paradigms, 89
　fragmentation of, 3–5, 30–31, 48–49, 119
　mass society, 1, 50–51
Human nature, 17–18, 35, 36
Human relations, 125–26, 130
Hume, David, 177n.
Hunter, Floyd, 174n., 176n.
Husserl, Edmund, 122, 178n.

Ideal types, 95–97

Jackson, Jay M., 171n.
James, William, 122, 123, 175n., 178n.
Jaspers, Karl, 170n.
Jordan, Elijah, 59, 171n.

Kaplan, Abraham, 87, 171n., 173n., 175n., 176n.
Katz, Daniel, 176n.
Kerr, Clark, 143–44, 145, 179n.
Kirk, Russell, 172n.
Kockelmans, Joseph, 178n.
Korzybski, Alfred, 175n.
Kroeber, Alfred L., 179n.
Kuhn, Thomas S., 88, 89, 147, 148, 174n., 176n., 180n.

Laing, R. D., 170n., 173n.
Langer, Susanne, 175n.
La Piere, Richard, 80, 176n.
Law, scientific, 77
Leadership
　autocratic, 116–17
　democratic, 116–17
　laissez-faire, 116–17
Leavitt, Harold, 177n.
LeBon, Gustave, 151, 152, 180n.
Levy, Marion, 40
Lewin, Kurt, 116, 117, 179n.
Liberation, problem of, 51, 64–65
Liebow, Elliot, 177n.
Lippitt, Ronald, 116, 117
Lipset, Seymour M., 110, 111, 171n.
Loomis, Charles P., 171n.
Luckmann, Thomas, 172n., 178n., 180n.
Lukacs, Gyorgy, 172n.
Lundberg, George A., 176n.

Machiavelli, Niccolo, 165–66, 180*n*.
MacIver, Robert, 94
MacPherson, C. B., 172*n*.
Malinowski, Branislaw, 40, 177*n*.
Manis, Jerome G., 178*n*.
Mannheim, Karl, 172*n*.
Marcel, Gabriel, 176*n*.
Maritain, Jacques, 55
Marriage, 40, 44–45
Martindale, Don, 173*n*., 178*n*.
Marx, Karl, 42–44, 48, 50, 53, 56, 62, 93, 94, 96, 160–61, 172*n*., 179*n*.
Marxism, 35, 42–44, 48
Maslow, Abraham, 40, 172*n*.
Mass mind, 150–53, 155
Mass society, 152
McCarthy, Joseph, 177*n*.
McGinniss, Joe, 170*n*., 171*n*.
Mead, George H., 48, 58, 122, 175*n*.
Mechanical solidarity, 96–97
Meisel, James H., 171*n*.
Meltzer, Bernard N., 178*n*.
Mental hospitals, 112–13
Merton, Robert K., 172*n*.
Michels, Robert, 110–11
Milgram, Sidney, 177*n*.
Mill, John Stuart, 175*n*.
Miller, David L., 178*n*.
Mills, C. Wright, 4, 20, 58, 87, 172*n*., 174*n*., 176*n*.
Monism, 40–46, 56–57, 94
Mosca, Gaetano, 48
Mukerjee, Radhakamal, 4, 59, 172*n*.
Multiversity, 143–45
Murray, John Courtney, 36, 37, 173*n*.

Natural law, 36–40, 55–56, 94
 Catholic tradition, 36–38, 40
Nieburg, H. L., 177*n*.
Nisbet, Robert, 172*n*.
Northrop, F. S. C., 59, 172*n*.
Novak, Michael, 171*n*.

Order, problem of, 50–51, 64–65
Organizations, 19–20, 23–25, 27, 51, 102, 107
 formal, 113–14
 informal, 102, 113–14
Ortega y Gasset, José, 170*n*., 172*n*.
Orwell, George, 175*n*.

Pappenheim, Fritz, 173*n*.
Paradigm, 88–89, 147–48
Pareto, Vilfredo, 48, 57
Parsons, Talcott, 40, 48, 50, 58, 94, 122, 170*n*., 174*n*., 176*n*.
Participant observation. *See* Social research, methods of
Pepper, Stephen, 172*n*.
Plato, 40, 158
Pluralism, 46–50, 57–58, 94
Process, 10, 16, 125–26

Process model, 50–53, 58–59
Propaganda, 5, 13, 46, 53, 66, 68–69, 71–72, 74–75, 76, 80, 82, 97, 104, 148–50, 154–55, 156
Public opinion, 12–13
Purpose, 136, 138

Questionnaire, 103, 120
 see also Social research, methods of
Quetelet, Adolphe, 98

Reflexive Sociology, 142–43
Relativization, 23–28, 104
Remmling, Gunter, 172*n*.
Reputational method. *See* Social research, methods of
Reynolds, Janice M., 177*n*.
Reynolds, Larry T., 177*n*.
Ridgeway, James, 179*n*.
Rieff, Philip, 171*n*.
Riesman, David, 94, 171*n*., 178*n*.
Roethlisberger, F. J., 177*n*.
Roles, 91, 98
Roose, Kenneth D., 179*n*.
Rose, Arnold M., 167, 175*n*.
Royce, Josiah, 172*n*.
Rumble, Wilfrid E., 174*n*.
Russell, Bertrand, 3, 170*n*., 171*n*.
Rytina, Joan Huber, 171*n*.

Saltzstein, Herbert D., 171*n*.
Sample, 104
Santayana, George, 174*n*.
Science, 5, 61, 67–68, 119
 applied, 67–68, 175*n*.
 human, 64, 81–82, 92, 162–69
 natural, 64, 77, 81, 88, 91–92, 162–63, 165–67, 169
 pure, 175*n*.
Scientific revolution. *See* Paradigm
Scott, W. Richard, 58
Self, 16, 17, 26, 121, 123
Self-understanding, 6–7, 52–53, 91, 101, 122, 132, 157, 159, 165
 liberal education, and, 133
Sereno, Renzo, 171*n*.
Shelley, Mary, 174*n*.
Simmel, Georg, 48, 57
Smith, Adam, 171*n*.
Smith, Don, 81, 176*n*.
Smith, Dusky Lee, 143, 179*n*.
Smith, Howard R., 171*n*.
Social engineering, 164
Social ethic. *See* Belongingness
Social problems, 40
Social research, methods of, 90–94, 120, 122
 case study, 110–11
 demographic, 98–99, 111–12
 depth interview, 105–7, 115–16
 experimental, 107–8, 116–17
 historical, 94–98, 110–11
 nonparticipant, 102–3, 113–14

 participant, 99–102, 112–13
 survey, 103–5, 114–15
Sociology, 127–29
 as control, 163–65
 as liberation, 163–65
 history of, 128–29
 humanistic, 139
 scope of, 127, 129
 of sociology, 148
Sorel, George, 171*n*.
Sorokin, Pitirim, 4, 59, 122, 172*n*., 174*n*., 177*n*., 178*n*.
Space, 133–35
 action, 134
 movement, 133–34
 transactional, 134–35
Spencer, Herbert, 94
Spinoza Baruch, 165–66, 180*n*.
Staude, John R., 179*n*.
Stoddard, Lothrop, 35
Storr, Anthony, 56
Stouffer, Samuel, 114, 115
Suicide, 98, 111–12
Sullivan, Harry Stack, 40
Sumner, William Graham, 178*n*.
Survey method. *See* Social research, methods of

Theory, social. *See* Social thought
Thomas, W. I., 173*n*.
Thorson, Thomas L., 176*n*.
Timasheff, Nicholas, 173*n*.
Time, 137–38
 action, 137
 movement, 137
 transactional, 137–38
Toennies, Ferdinand, 96, 176*n*.
Triplett, Randall, 179*n*.
Trow, Martin C., 110, 177*n*.

University. *See* Multiversity

Veblen, Thorstein, 56, 94
Velikovsky, Immanuel, 87–88, 176*n*.
Violence, 71–72

Walsh, Mary Elizabeth, 39, 40, 173
Warnock, Mary, 171*n*.
Webb, Eugene, 90, 176*n*., 177*n*.
Weber, Max, 48, 93, 94, 147, 176*n*., 180*n*.
Weinstein, Deena, 170*n*., 180*n*.
Weinstein, Michael A., 170*n*., 172*n*., 178*n*.
White, Ralph, 116, 117
Whyte, William F., 20, 22, 177*n*.
Whyte, William H., Jr., 172*n*.
Williams, Robin M., Jr., 144, 179*n*.
Women's liberation movement, 44

Zetterberg, Hans L., 175*n*.
Znaniecki, Florian, 58, 122, 140, 179*n*.